The DIY Bride

The DIY Bride

40 FUN PROJECTS FOR YOUR ULTIMATE
ONE-OF-A-KIND WEDDING

Khris Cochran

The Taunton Press

A STONESONG PRESS BOOK

This book is dedicated to Jason, the best husband a girl could ever hope for.

The Taunton Press
Inspiration for hands-on living®

The Taunton Press, Inc., 63 South Main Street, PO Box 5506, Newtown, CT 06470-5506
e-mail: tp@taunton.com

Editor: Katie Benoit
Jacket/Cover design: 3+Co.
Cover illustration: Asami Mitsuhira/3+Co.
Interior design/Layout: 3+Co.
A Stonesong Press Book
Illustrator: Jim Starr
Photographer: Jack Deutsch

Library of Congress Cataloging-in-Publication Data
Cochran, Khris.
 The DIY bride : 40 fun projects for your ultimate one-of-a-kind wedding / Khris Cochran.
     p. cm.
 "A Stonesong Press Book."
 Includes bibliographical references and index.
 ISBN 978-1-56158-964-7 (alk. paper)
 1. Handicraft. 2. Weddings--Equipment and supplies. 3. Wedding decorations. I. Title.

TT149.C583 2007
745.92'6--dc22
                         2007023517
Printed in Singapore
10 9 8 7 6 5 4 3 2 1

The following manufacturers/names appearing in *The DIY Bride* are trademarks: Adobe Illustrator™, Adobe Photoshop™, Avery®, Band-Aids®, Barbie®, CorelDRAW®, E6000®, Easy-Bake®, eBay®, EnviroTex Lite®, Fabri-Tac®, Fiskars®, Gem-Tac®, Google™, Hobby Lobby®, iPod™, Lucite®, Michael's®, Microsoft Paint™, Microsoft® Publisher, Microsoft® Word, Play-Doh®, Popsicle®, Styrofoam®, Swarovski®, Target®, The Print Shop™, View-Master®, Wal-Mart®, X-Acto®

ACKNOWLEDGMENTS

Behind this book stands an awesome group of people who helped bring it to life. I would never have undertaken this project without their help and support.

At The Stonesong Press, I thank Alison Fargis and Ellen Scordato for their tireless hand-holding and gentle guidance while I made my way through writing copy and creating crafts as a first-time author. My deepest appreciation goes to Alison for bringing me this opportunity and for her endless patience. Her feedback, skillful editing, and overall enthusiasm for this project will never be forgotten. I'd be remiss not to thank the ever-fabulous Ellen, whose keen eye for detail is extraordinary. Everything she touched—words and photos—is better because of it.

My sincerest thanks to Katie Benoit, my brilliant editor and cheerleader, Wendi Mijal, Chris Thompson, Carol Singer, and the entire crew at The Taunton Press who made this book possible. Hearty thanks to Jack Deutsch, photographer extraordinaire, who beautifully captured each image, and to brilliant stylist Laura Maffeo, who took my crafts and used her magic to turn them into art. Thank you to Matt Lewis and Renato Poliafito at Baked in Red Hook, Brooklyn, who provided the gorgeous (not to mention delicious!) cakes and cupcakes you see in the photos. Also thank you to Eleanor Ambos at the enchanting Metropolitan Building in Long Island City, Queens.

A big shout out goes to my family and friends for their unconditional love and support. You guys rock! (But you already knew that.)

A special thank you to my mother-in-law, Blythe, who's not only my rubber-stamping guru, but who's directly responsible for my foray into wedding crafts. Without her, I wouldn't be doing this.

An eternal thank you to my husband, Jason, who supported me throughout this entire process in every way he could. For graciously putting up with piles of craft paraphernalia around the house, for those late-night runs to the craft store, for listening to me when I was at my wit's end (many times), for being my Sherpa on cross-country photo shoots, and for believing in my abilities. I am the luckiest girl to have him.

contents

introduction

Do you consider yourself a crafter? I never did. But I found that producing beautiful, personal, unique items for my own wedding was one of the most satisfying things I've ever done— and I wrote this book so you can do the same.

What is it that makes brides want to get involved in crafting the details of their wedding: the clever invites, the inspired centerpieces, the tasty favors, the funky place cards? Some artsy gals do it 'cause they love being hands-on and can't turn down the opportunity to let their talents shine. Others want to make sure the elements of their wedding are deeply personal and truly unique. (Let's face it—who wants a bland, run-of-the-mill wedding? The absolute best weddings are the ones where the couple shines through in each and every detail, aren't they?) Some brides-to-be are super-budget-conscious. I've found that most wedding crafters are a bit of all three.

So if I wasn't a crafter, how'd I get here? I've always been kind of crafty, but my real skills lie in dissection and reassembly. Taking things apart, learning how

they're made, and then putting them back together has fascinated me since early childhood.

While other girls were dressing their Barbies®, I was exploring the innards of her remote-controlled Corvette. When other girls were playing dress-up in their mom's eveningwear, I was creating fabulous frocks from my very own dresses with scissors, a stapler, and indelible markers—much to the horror of my parents. Throughout my adolescence and adult life I crafted out of necessity, usually for quick fixes to small problems. Missing handles on a hand-me-down dresser? Hot glue and pieces of found coral worked beautifully as funky substitutes. Ugly blades on a ceiling fan in a rental apartment? Double-stick tape and a cut-up paper parasol made for a lovely disguise. All these things were crafty, sure, but I never considered myself a crafter.

Crafters were an entirely different breed—artsy and uber-talented. I just threw odds 'n ends together to survive college-induced poverty or to avert potential party crises.

So, what made me a crafter? I was a bride on a budget. I became engaged to a lovely man named Jason and started planning my dream day for October 2000. Armed with stacks of glossy bridal magazines, I pored through every page. Although much didn't fit our personalities or style, I bought into the prepackaged ideal wedding hook, line, and sinker. This was, after all, what weddings were "supposed" to look and be like. I had not the slightest idea what any of these precious details would cost, but I did know that I had to have these wonderful things for my wedding to be perfect.

But then my fiancé and I established a budget. It was far less than I expected it would be, even with generous financial donations from the parents. And I realized my dream day—that one when the whole universe stops, realigns, and spins around me—wasn't going to happen the way the wedding magazines, bridal salons, and slick advertisements told me I was entitled to.

But the world did not end, my friends. My ever-level-headed fiancé was more philosophical about the whole thing. First, I was being a brat (this was before "bridezilla" was ever in the cultural lexicon). Second, our wedding needed to be about us and not about

someone else's vision of what our wedding should be. And third, we were resourceful enough to stretch our budget as far as we needed to. He was absolutely right on all accounts. We knew what we had to do. It was time to get our craft on!

With renewed interest in all-things wedding, Jason and I, as a unified couple, set out to create a new plan for a posh, personal wedding on a budget we could afford. As a result, my wedding was one of the best I've ever been to. The same results can happen for you. Don't be shy, my friends. Take it from me, a once timid and reluctant crafter, you can do this and have fun, too! First, prioritize what's important to you. Ceremony or reception? Favors or decoration? Attire or transportation? Once you work out on which items you want to spend time and/or money, you're better able to determine how much to budget for each thing. That's exactly what we did.

To stay on budget, Jason and I opted to try making some of the simpler wedding items. Yet very few templates and how-to instructions for do-it-yourself wedding crafts existed, and those available were usually very basic and not the right fit for our wedding. We started most of our crafts from scratch and relied heavily on my predilection for pulling things apart and seeing how they tick. We jumped right into my pile of magazine clippings and crafted mock-ups of our favorite ideas but added our own twists and style. That semi-cute invitation with a simple vellum overlay turned into a funky, gold harlequin print card with vellum overlay. Those fancy white bon-bon boxes were made in transparent purple and green papers and held delicious, colorful petit fours. Individual cakes as centerpieces from a trés chic bakery were interpreted as beautifully decorated cupcakes nestled on a shimmery glass pedestal on each table.

We had a blast crafting our wedding projects and loved bringing in our friends and families to lend a hand. My future mother-in-law taught me all about rubber stamping. A gal pal showed me where to find unique papers. Another friend shared her in-depth knowledge of typography and page layout. We had our friends and family come together to assemble, sort, and generally make things happen for us. All of these things not only helped us stay within our budget but also made our wedding experience meaningful and uniquely ours. Our wedding came and went with nary a problem, and to this day we're glad we did it ourselves.

As we experimented with designs and ideas, I began sharing our triumphs, failures, and near-misses with local online bridal support groups. The response was overwhelming! Soon, I was being asked for templates and directions for every project I made. Other brides started openly sharing their designs and ideas,

too. Word spread quickly, and DIYBride.com was started to handle all of the requests and to facilitate templates, designs, and ideas being passed from bride to bride.

The DIY Bride is testimony to the fact that anyone —whether she's a crafter or not—can create a lush wedding on any budget, no matter what her skills. And your wedding can be *yours*, not a cookie-cutter magazine version of a wedding. All that's needed are some helping hands, simple tools, good instruction, and a sense of adventure.

Whether you're a first-time do-it-yourselfer or a pro, there are projects in this book that you can easily make and adapt to your own personal style. In most cases, all of the supplies can be found in any metropolitan area. For those harder-to-find items, we have a handy resources section in the back that will tell you where to order your goods.

This book combines lessons learned in crafting from my own wedding and the DIY wedding goodness I've amassed over the years. With each project, I share tips and hints to make the craft easier and show ways to make it uniquely yours. For those who like to comparison shop, you'll see cost comparisons between the DIY version and what you'd pay retail for a similar product. Is the savings worth the effort? You can decide before you invest time or money. And you don't have to craft these projects alone! Check out the sidebars for how to use the projects to gather your pals together for a little crafty fun.

If you find yourself needing a little extra help and inspiration, do visit the DIYBride.com community, where we sponsor DIY get-togethers and ongoing classes and seminars, bringing together the bridal community and sharing our knowledge and support. It's a great party—even before the wedding.

Happy crafting!

THE BASICS *Tools & Techniques*

I'm a reformed gadget queen. Early in my crafty beginnings, if a tool was new or improved—or just plain bright 'n' shiny—it had to be mine. I'd drag home the latest sleek and slick goodies, my head filled with dreams of the effortless and efficient crafting I'd surely soon be doing. Most purchases never delivered on their promises, and they were quickly retired to a shelf in my craft space affectionately known as the gadget graveyard.

Over the years I stripped my crafter's toolkit down to the bare essentials. It's the best thing I did to boost my productivity, save money, and free up much-needed space in my craft area.

When getting started as a crafter, it's easy to be lured into buying the sexiest, prettiest, most expensive tools on the market. But you know what? They're really not necessary. All you need is a good basic collection of tools to prepare you for nearly any wedding craft you wish to tackle.

Most common craft tools and supplies are found at local stores or online. Major craft retailers such as Michael's® and Hobby Lobby® carry a large collection of basic tools and supplies. Large discount department stores like Target® and Wal-Mart® now have whole areas dedicated to crafts products. And don't forget the online craft universe. The web is full of specialty stores that offer an abundance of affordable products. The resources section of this book features a handy list of great retailers to help you on your search for the best tools on a budget.

Essential Tools and Supplies

A well-stocked tool kit will make your crafting life easier. The right tool for each project simplifies your task at hand and, as a bonus, helps you achieve pro-quality results.

The tools recommended in this section will help you build a basic tool kit that'll carry you through all of the projects in this book and beyond.

Adhesives

Double-sided tape This clear tape has adhesive on both sides for quick and easy bonding. It adheres instantly and will not bleed through or buckle paper. Use it in place of glue for paper projects.

Fabric glue Don't sew? No problem! Use this liquid adhesive for permanent fabric-to-fabric bonds. It will dry stiff but can be softened with a warm iron without losing its hold.

Glue gun and glue sticks Trigger-fed glue guns heat solid glue sticks and dispense the melted glue. They provide an instant bond and are perfect for adhering nonpaper materials such as silk flowers, lace, ribbon, and more for craft projects. (Caution: Hot glue will sometimes bleed through lightweight papers.)

Spray adhesive An aerosol glue, spray adhesive is one of my favorite tools for crafting. It's best used for adhering paper to paper or paper to fabric. It creates a permanent bond, adheres very quickly, and dries clear. Remember to always use in a well-ventilated space.

Cutting Tools

Craft knife Also known by the brand name X-Acto® knife, this pencil-like tool has a sharp, single-edged blade at the end. It's best for cutting ornate designs on paper, vellum, and other light materials. Heavy-duty versions are also available for cutting thicker materials such as chipboard and balsa wood.

Cutting mat Self-healing cutting mats are used in conjunction with craft knives and rotary cutters. Their smooth surface repairs itself after a cut, leaving an even cutting area for your next project. Most feature ruled lines on the surface to make cutting and measuring a snap.

Paper cutter Use this tool for making straight cuts on paper. Most styles have either a simple sliding blade or a rotary blade, with built-in measuring grids and/or rulers.

Rotary cutter A rotary cutter looks and acts much like a pizza wheel. It will cut fabric or paper as it rolls over the surface, which allows you to make a long, straight cut in a single movement.

Scissors A good pair of general-purpose scissors will make your life easier. Invest in the best pair you can afford. A good pair with stainless steel blades will last decades with minimum maintenance. Scissors with a blade length of 5 inches to 8 inches will be suitable for most craft projects.

Rubber Stamping

Art stamps Using art stamps is an easy way to add graphics to your projects. There are two common types of art stamps on the market: rubber and acrylic. Rubber stamps are opaque; acrylic stamps are transparent. Both types will imprint images, words, or patterns on nearly any surface and are available in countless designs and sizes.

Embossing powders Made from a powder-like plastic material, embossing powders are sprinkled over pigment inks and melted with a heat tool to create a raised impression on paper, metal, or wood. Embossing powders are available in dozens of colors and metallic finishes. The powders can be found at craft stores, scrapbook shops, and online rubber stamp retailers.

Heat embossing tool This handy gadget is used to melt embossing powders on your paper crafts. There are two common types: the bullet style, which is shaped like a standard flashlight, and the hair dryer style, which looks like a mini blow-dryer. Both perform the same function, so select the one that's easiest for you to handle. The result is a shiny, raised (embossed) impression.

Ink Ink is used with an ink pad for rubber stamps. Thousands of ink colors are on the market, available from several manufacturers. Although there are several types of inks to choose from, two types will carry you through the majority of your stamp projects:

Dye Inks Dye-based inks are water-based, permanent inks. They dry quickly and can be used on all paper types. Because of their fast drying time, they are not suitable for embossing.

Pigment Ink Pigment-based inks are thicker, more vibrant, and slower to dry than dye-based inks. They can be used on any paper but will smudge when wet. Their slow drying time makes them perfect for use with embossing powders.

11

Jewelry Making

Round-nose pliers These pliers have rounded ends. They're used for creating smooth loops in jewelry wire.

Wire cutters A good wire cutter is essential for all wire projects. The preferred style for jewelry projects is the flush-cutting or side-flush-cutting wire cutter because it creates a flat cut. Household wire cutters are often heavier than flush jewelry cutters and they tend to leave a jagged edge. Like a good pair of scissors, they'll last for years and require little maintenance. Buy the best pair you can afford.

Paper Crafts

Bone folder Bone folders are used to smooth, score, and crease paper. Traditionally, they were made of polished cow bone. Today you can find heavy acrylic versions at craft and stationery stores.

Eyelets Eyelets are small metal rings used to reinforce holes in fabric or paper. They're available in a wide assortment of colors and sizes, making them a fun embellishment for invitations and programs.

Eyelet setter This tool crimps the back of an eyelet to hold it in place. When selecting a setter, buy one that offers attachments to accommodate different sizes of eyelets. Many styles of setter require the use of a hammer. If yours doesn't come packaged with a hammer, a regular household hammer can be used.

Hole punches A vast array of paper punches are available. From simple holes to ornate designs, you can find thousands of shapes to fit your style.

Sewing Equipment

All-purpose thread This polyester or cotton-wrapped polyester thread is used for hand and machine sewing on most fabrics.

Iron A heavy-duty household iron is essential for all of your fabric projects.

Needles For hand-sewn projects, have on hand a selection of needle sizes. Most needles are sold in variety packs of 10–50 for your convenience.

Pins Use pins with plastic or glass heads; they're easier to see.

General

In addition to the specialty tools above, I recommend the following tools that you're probably already familiar with:

- **No. 2 pencils**
- **Cellophane tape**
- **Emery boards**
- **Extra craft knife blades**
- **Gum erasers** (these are softer and less abrasive than regular erasers)

- **Hammer**
- **Permanent markers**
- **Ruler and straightedge**
- **Sponge paintbrushes**
- **White pencil**

Techniques

If you're new to crafting, some of the techniques mentioned in this book may seem a little intimidating. Don't worry! Most of the projects have been designed specifically for a first-time or novice crafter.

To help you navigate your way to a successful project, here is an introduction to the basic techniques used in this book.

USING A BONE FOLDER

1. Score the paper or card with the tip of the bone folder. Scoring creates a line or depression in the paper that will help the paper fold.

2. Fold the paper along the crease you just made and gently press flat.

3. With the bone folder held perpendicular to the paper, smooth the edge of the broad side of the bone folder along the fold with slight pressure. This will make a crisp fold in the paper.

USING A RUBBER STAMP

1. Tap the surface of the rubber stamp onto an ink pad. Be gentle! It doesn't take a lot of pressure to ink a stamp. If you press too hard or rub the stamp along the surface of the ink pad, you'll get too much ink on your stamp and ruin your pads. Too much ink will bleed through your paper or smudge the image.

2. Hold the stamp firmly and press down on the paper or card. Do not rock or move the stamp. If you do, you'll smudge your image.

3. Lift the stamp straight up.

4. After you're done stamping, clean your stamp per the manufacturer's recommendations.

HEAT EMBOSSING A STAMPED IMAGE

1. Stamp an image onto paper using pigment ink.

2. Immediately cover the entire stamped image with a layer of embossing powder.

3. Shake the excess powder off the stamped image onto a scrap piece of paper. Return the excess powder to the jar.

4. Turn on your heat embossing tool and allow it to heat up for a few seconds.

5. Hold the heated tool over the embossed image, moving the tool back and forth to evenly heat the paper. The embossing powder will begin to melt and become shiny. When all of the embossing powder has melted, turn off the heat tool and set the paper aside to cool.

SETTING EYELETS

1. Place paper onto a self-healing mat.

2. Use a small circle hole punch the size of your eyelet or the punch end of an eyelet-setting tool to make a hole in your paper. (Tip: If using an eyelet-setting tool, hit the end of the tool with a hammer to punch a hole.)

3. Place the eyelet into the hole you just made so that the top side of the eyelet is on the front side of the paper.

4. Turn the paper over so that the top of the eyelet is facing down. Position the eyelet-setting tool over the eyelet and hit the end of the tool with a small hammer. The back of the eyelet will spread out. Remove the eyelet tool and completely flatten the back of the eyelet with the hammer, if needed.

CREATING A BASIC WIRE JEWELRY LOOP

1. Place beads on a head pin, eye pin, or other wire. Leave ¼ inch of wire above the top of the last bead.

2. Use your fingers to bend the wire against the last bead at a right angle.

3. Grab the end of the wire with round-nose pliers.

4. Roll the wire into a complete circle by rotating your wrist.

5. To rotate the wire all the way around, just readjust your grip. Make sure you grab the wire at the same point on the pliers to ensure an even loop.

Proper Project Planning
FOR THE
Big Day

Creating do-it-yourself projects for your wedding may seem a bit daunting, whether you're a seasoned crafter or a total newbie to the world of cardstock and glue guns. There's a lot to do and a limited time to complete all of it. But don't fret! You can do all of the projects you want with some simple planning.

A detailed schedule of tasks will save your sanity during this frenzied time. The earlier you begin planning, the sooner you can get into action and finish all of those projects. Look for these informative icons throughout:

Going Solo: These crafts are ideal for a DIY Bride-to-be.

Party Time: Get your wedding party together; you may need all hands on deck for these crafts.

It's a Girl Thing: These are fun crafts you and your girlfriends can create together.

Family Bonding: Whether it's Mom, your flower girl, or your future mother-in-law, you can connect with your family over these projects.

Couple's Corner: What better way to bond with your sweetie than over a hot glue gun?

Made for Your Maid: These are projects you'll want to hand off to one of your bridesmaids to complete the day before or the morning of your wedding day.

Where the Boys Are: We DIY chicks are more than capable of doing the heavy lifting, but why break a sweat when you have hunky groomsmen around? Put them to work!

I've created a craft timeline to help break down your to-do list into manageable chunks.

AS SOON AS POSSIBLE

☐ Pick a wedding date and secure your wedding and reception venues.

☐ Select the color scheme or theme of your wedding.

☐ Decide on an approximate number of guests to invite.

8 MONTHS OR MORE AHEAD

☐ Compile a list of all the do-it-yourself projects you'll create.

☐ For each project, create a list of supplies you'll need. Start looking for sales and coupons at your local craft supply stores. Buy tools and supplies on sale when you can throughout the year.

Tip: Many craft stores have sales right before major holidays.

☐ If using professional engagement shots in any of your projects (save-the-dates or invitations, for example), schedule a shoot with your photographer.

6 MONTHS TO 8 MONTHS AHEAD

- ☐ Compile a list of out-of-town guests.
- ☐ Design the save-the-date cards.
- ☐ Buy supplies for the save-the-date cards.
- ☐ If you have overseas guests, send the save-the-dates 6 to 8 months before the wedding to allow for delivery time through local postal services.
- ☐ Send save-the-date cards 6 months in advance of your wedding date to all other guests.

4 TO 6 MONTHS AHEAD

- ☐ Many of the projects in this book are great for groups (just look for the handy-dandy "Party Time" icon). Because helping hands will make it easier for you to get the larger projects done more quickly, start planning crafting parties with your wedding crew early to get bulk projects done and out of the way. Try to schedule one work party for each group-friendly project to prevent yourself from getting bridal burnout.
- ☐ Buy supplies for invitations, thank-you cards, favors, programs, and any other projects that your group will tackle together.
- ☐ Design and print invitations.

Tip: Set aside a half an hour each day to work on your projects. It's manageable and you'll be amazed at how much you can accomplish in 30 minutes.

2 TO 4 MONTHS AHEAD

- ☐ Send invitations 8 weeks before your wedding.
- ☐ Purchase supplies for remaining nonperishable craft projects.

1 TO 2 MONTHS AHEAD

- ☐ Complete jewelry, accessories, and wedding décor projects.
- ☐ Design and print thank-you cards.

2 TO 4 WEEKS AHEAD

- ☐ Design and print wedding programs.
- ☐ Place orders for flowers and herbs to be delivered 3 days before wedding.

1 TO 2 WEEKS AHEAD

- ☐ Get final guest count. Make place cards and favor packaging for each guest.
- ☐ Make seating chart.

1 TO 2 DAYS AHEAD

- ☐ Purchase supplies for fudge favors.
- ☐ Make the fudge, cut into squares, and refrigerate overnight.
- ☐ Pick up (or have delivered) flowers and herbs for any floral projects.
- ☐ Assemble floral projects the day before the wedding.
- ☐ Assemble the fudge favors and package them the day before the wedding.

WEDDING DAY

- ☐ Assemble the Buds and Blossoms Bridal Bag.
- ☐ Assemble the Herb Boutonnieres.
- ☐ Assemble the Stephanotis Ring Pillow.
- ☐ Hang the Pew Cones on the chairs or pews.
- ☐ Set up the Hanging Garden Aisle Markers.
- ☐ Set up the Ceremony Canopy.
- ☐ Set up the centerpieces and table numbers at the reception.

POST WEDDING

- ☐ Send any thank-you cards for gifts received at (or after) the wedding.
- ☐ Gather wedding mementos for shadowboxes and scrapbooks.

1 Telling the World

Save-the-Dates, Invitations & Thank Yous

You're getting married and want to shout it from the rooftops! Although it might be fun to do, it's not the best way to get the word out to your friends and family…unless they live within shouting distance. An easier way to spread the good news is through good old-fashioned snail mail. Whether they are save-the-dates (a handy way of getting guests to pencil in your big day on their calendar), invitations (a perfect way to spell out the details on your upcoming nuptials), or thank you notes (the best way to thank guests for their wonderful thoughtful gifts), this chapter provides the skinny on spreading your good news without annoying your neighbors.

Save the Date!

Please join us as we celebrate our wedding by the sea in the beautiful city of Santa Barbara, California.

Please mark your calendars and plan to arrive a few days early for weekend-long celebrations.

Thomas King + Amanda Leung

will celebrate their marriage on
Saturday, May 16, 2009

Ty Warner Sea Center
Santa Barbara, CA

Formal invitation and travel information to follow.

SHAKE IT UP! *Save-the-Date Card*

I'm a sucker for flashy and gimmicky cards. Anything that moves, makes noise, or features a touch of glitter is pure crafty goodness in my book. This save-the-date, a shaker card, is a huge hit with students in my card-making classes and is one of my personal favorites to make for special occasions. Because there are very few standards for their etiquette and design, save-the-dates are perfect candidates for a bit of frivolity and fun.

Shaker cards, for the uninitiated, feature a raised window on the surface of the card that holds moving filler of some sort. You can use any small objects as filler: beads, sand, glitter, confetti, seeds—let your imagination go wild with this one!

The card featured here is perfect for an elegant beach wedding, with its subtle color palette, sand, and a single sea star. Not the beachy type? No problem!

Heading to Vegas? Try using a playing card in the background and tiny dice and confetti as the filler. Planning an informal garden wedding? Use seeds or dried flowers. A winter wedding? Clear glitter and snowflakes punched from a sheet of vellum paper are stunning.

You'll love this project because it's easily adaptable to any theme and is easy to make. Your guests will love it because it's unexpected and a whole lot of fun.

My friends, Daphne and Mark, after many years of living together, decided to get married. Their save-the-date played up their longtime reluctance to tie the knot. "We swore it would never happen. We held off for as long as we could. But, hey, we changed our minds. Save the date for our May '04 wedding in beautiful Carmel-by-the-Sea."

Get Your Craft On:

Party Time!

Helping hands will make this project easy-peasy. Get your bridesmaids, groomsmen, and family members together and divide labor into the following stations:

Supplies Needed

- 1 sheet of light blue cardstock, cut to 4¼ inches by 5½ inches, for the back
- 1 sheet of ivory cardstock, cut to 3¾ inches by 5 inches, for the save-the-date wording
- 1 sheet of light green cardstock, cut to 3¾ inches by 5 inches, for the window frame
- 1 sheet of transparency film, cut to 3¾ inches by 5 inches, for the window
- Double-stick tape
- Double-sided foam adhesive strips, less than ¼ inches wide
- Shells or other extras
- Craft sand
- Craft knife
- Computer

STATION 1: Cutting This group kicks off the fun. Have them measure and cut all of the cardstock to appropriate sizes.

STATION 2: Window This group adheres the window sheets to the frames and places the foam tape on top of the transparencies.

STATION 3: Backing This group adheres the printed save-the-date wording onto the backing pieces of cardstock.

STATION 4: Final Assembly Almost done! This group adheres the frames and backing pieces together, inserts the sand and shells, and seals everything together.

STATION 5: Envelopes These lucky helpers get to address envelopes, place the save-the-date cards inside, and affix postage.

DIRECTIONS

1. Let's get started! Open Microsoft® Word™ and create a new document. From the File menu, click on Page Setup, then click on the Paper tab. Select Custom Page Size from the Paper Size options. Set the custom page size for 3¾ inches wide by 5 inches tall. Click OK.

2. Next, let's set the margins. From the File menu, click on Page Setup, then click on the Margins tab. Set the margin spacing to 0.25 inch for all margins, left, right, top, and bottom. Insert your save-the-date wording, save, and print onto ivory cardstock. Be creative with your wording! These save-the-dates are your opportunity to let your personalities shine.

3. Adhere the printed ivory cardstock on top of the light blue cardstock with double-stick tape. Make sure it is centered and level. Set it aside.

4. Next, make the frame. The frame will be raised by the foam tape, creating a 3-D pocket and allowing you to insert the filler. On the back side of the light green cardstock draw a straight line from top to bottom and side to side ¼ inch from the edge on each of the sides. Using a straight edge and a craft knife, cut along the pencil marks and remove the center (drawing a).

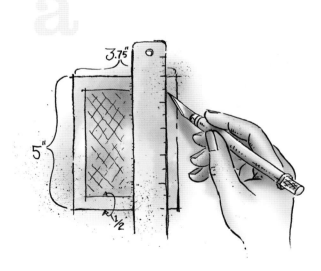

5. Still working on the back side of the light green cardstock, run a line of double-stick tape near the inner edges of the frame (drawing b).

6. Place the transparency sheet on top of the adhesive, pressing the transparency firmly in place. Caution! If there are any gaps where the transparency and adhesive meet, the sand and inclusions will leak (drawing c).

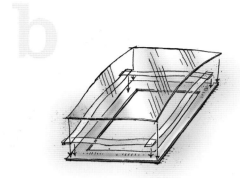

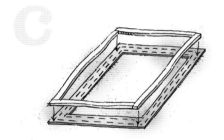

7. On top of the transparency, place strips of the double-sided foam tape near the inner edges of the frame but not right to the edge. Go in just a little bit, about ⅛ inch, so that the foam tape won't be visible through the window when the card is put together. Make sure there are no gaps or openings between the edges of the foam strips and the foam on the frame. Leave the protective lining on the surface of the tape until you are certain there are no gaps, otherwise the tape will attract all sorts of lint and debris.

8. Once the foam tape is secure, remove the protective lining on the left and right sides and the bottom. Leave the top lining in place (photo d).

9. Place the window frame piece on top of the back piece you made earlier, centering the window area over the save-the-date wording. Once the frame is lined up, press down firmly to secure the three sides of the frame.

10. You're doing great! At this stage, the top side of the frame should be open and not adhered to the backing. This will allow you to insert the sand and shells into the window box. Use a spoon to pour in the sand (you'll need a little less than a teaspoon per card), then drop the shell in.

11. Remove the lining on the top piece of foam tape and press the frame firmly into place. That wasn't so bad, was it? You now have a one-of-a-kind save-the-date to dazzle your nearest and dearest.

Tips & Hints:

- Foam tape is often cheapest at home improvement stores, where it can be purchased in large rolls.

- Make a template of the frame. Use it to trace the frame onto larger sheets of cardstock so you don't have to make exact measurements for each cut. You'll waste less paper and save time.

- Cut all of your cardstock pieces first. This helps speed the assembly.

- You can use bulkier items as filler by simply layering the foam tape to make the pocket deeper. However, sending bulkier items through the post can be more expensive, and the cards may get crushed in transit if sent in regular envelopes.

This Vegas-themed save-the-date card makes for a fun alternate design.

Cost Comparison

Retail costs for this kind of card varies widely. Expect to pay anywhere from $3 to $8 each for a generic shaker card. Make that more if you're looking for it to be customized. The DIY Bride version costs about $0.60 each when made in bulk.

Store Cost:	Your Cost:
$3-8	60¢

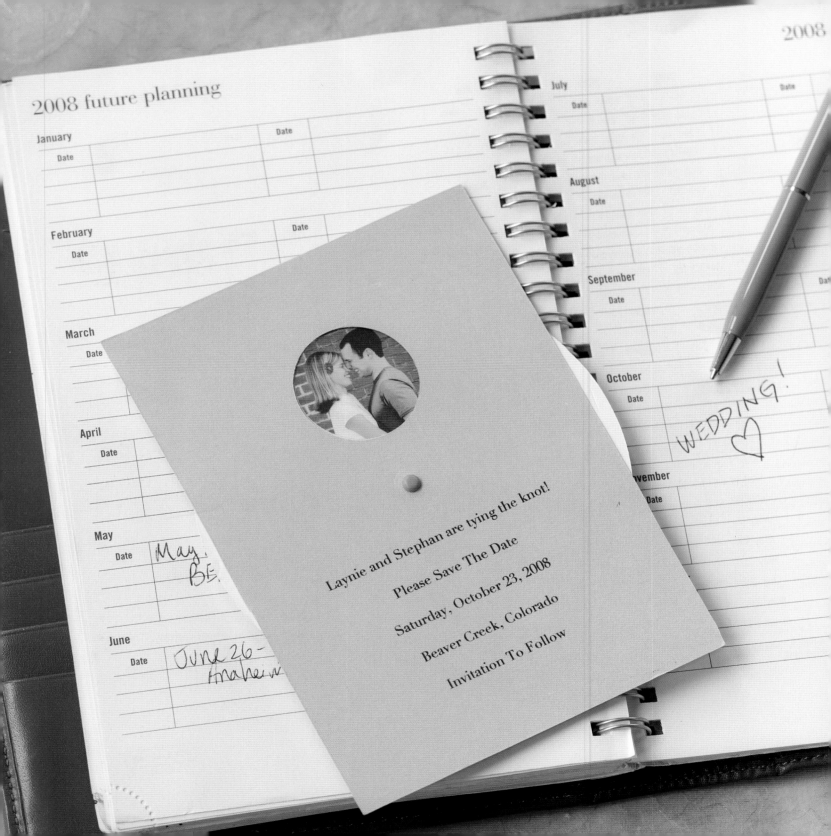

THE VIEWFINDER *Save-the-Date Card*

Retro toys rock my world, especially those from my 1970s childhood. Princess Leia action figures, Easy-Bake® ovens, Play-Doh®—they all make me a little a little weak in the knees. One of my favorites, however, was the View-Master®. I just loved the little picture discs that slipped into the binocular-like viewer. What new and exciting image would appear as the disc turned? A lion? The Eiffel Tower? A 3-D flower? Oh, sure, the images were a little cheesy, but that's what made them so charming.

Don't be afraid to show your playful and creative side in your save-the-dates! Your friends and family know you're not a bore so why bother with stuffy wedding stationery that's just not you? Not only will your guests love this unexpected bit of whimsy, but you'll let that stellar personality of yours shine through.

This playful save-the-date pays homage to the kitschy and fun View-Master toy. Though the directions include many steps, it is an easy project. Gather together your wedding party to lend a hand with assembly. It'll make the project go quickly.

Many hands make light work. Gather your best buds and fave family members together for a light lunch and some heavy crafting. Divide and conquer!

Supplies Needed

- 2 pieces of cardstock in the color of your choice, cut to 4 inches by 5½ inches
- 1 piece of white cardstock, 8½ inches by 11 inches
- 1 scanned or digital picture of you and your fiancé, or any other images you may want in the viewfinder, all approximately 1¼ inch by 1¼ inch
- Avery® White Sticker Project Paper
- Metal brad, $5/16$ inch
- Fiskars® Circle Cutter
- Circle punch, 1¼ inch diameter
- Computer with Microsoft Word
- Inkjet or laser printer

STATION 1: Front and Back Pieces

Get the party rolling with measuring and cutting the front and back pieces of cardstock.

STATION 2: Wheels

This group needn't reinvent the wheel, just cut 'em out of the cardstock.

STATION 3: Window Cutting

Your pals at lucky Station 3 get to cut the windows in the front panels of cardstock.

STATION 4: Hole Punching

For those who require lightweight projects (the elderly, the young, and the hung-over), set them to the task of punching small holes in the wheels and front panels.

STATION 5: Assembly

Put your most dexterous pals on the assembly line. They're in charge of putting together the front panels, wheels, and back panels.

STATION 6: Stickers

This station is for the chatty. They'll have a blast punching out the stickers while they catch up on the latest gossip.

STATION 7: Final Assembly

Find out who among your tribe has the best eye-hand coordination. This group places the stickers on the wheels.

CARD DIRECTIONS

1. From a sheet of cardstock, cut two pieces 4 inches by 5½ inches. One will be the front of your card. The other will be the back.

2. Create the printed front of the card. Open Microsoft Word and create a new document. From the File menu, click on Page Setup, and then click on the Paper tab. Select Custom Page Size from the Paper Size options. Set the custom page size for 4 inches wide by 5½ inches. Click OK.

3. For the margin spacing, click on the File menu again, click on Page Setup, and then click on the Margins tab. Set the margin spacing to 0.25 inch for the left and right margins. For the top and bottom, set the margin spacing to 0.50 inch.

4. From the Drawing toolbar in Word, create a text box in the lower half of the page, about 2¼ inches by 3 inches in size. Center it between the right and left margins. The top half of your document will remain blank. You'll later cut a window in that area.

5. Double-click the text box to pull up the Format Text Box menu. Under the Colors and Lines tab, change the Fill setting to No Fill and the Line setting to No Line. Click OK.

6. Click inside the text box and insert your save-the-date text. Don't be afraid to play around with different fonts, color choices, and text alignments here! Mixing and matching font types is a chic way to add a little somethin' to your card. Use a simple font, such as Arial, for the wording, but use a fine script font for your names. Or use a plain font for the entire save-the-date and bold the important stuff like your names and the date and location. Little touches go a long way. Format the text with your chosen font selections and any clip art you wish to include.

7. Save your front panel document and print onto cardstock. It's always a good idea to print a sample copy on a piece of scrap paper before you commit to the more expensive stuff.

8. After you print your front panels, punch a window on the front. To do this, insert the top of the cardstock into the slot on the 1¼-inch paper punch, making certain the window will be centered between the left and right sides of the cardstock (drawing a). Press the lever on the punch to cut the circle. If you find your punch is losing its mojo, fold some aluminum foil into a square and punch a few holes into it. The foil will sharpen your punch.

9. Next, create the wheel from a sheet of white cardstock. Use the circle cutter to cut a circle, 4¼ inches in diameter, in the card stock. A common problem with circle cutters is that they don't always cut through the entire circle in one turn. Don't worry! This usually happens when the cutting surface isn't totally flat. Just move your cutting area to a new, level table space. (Have some extra cardstock on hand, just in case you get incomplete cuts.)

10. Find the center of the circle and poke a small hole, large enough for the metal brad to slide through. Confession time: this is one of my favorite parts of this project. There's something oddly satisfy ing about poking holes in paper. Go figure. An easy way to find the center is to cut a 4¼-inch circle from a scrap piece of paper. Fold it in half from top to bottom and then in half again from left to right. Where the fold lines connect—the point—is the center. Use this as a template for placing holes in your cardstock. Lay it over your cardstock circles and use a pushpin, needle, or nail to make a small hole.

11. Make a hole in the front panel you printed earlier. Poke a hole 2⅝ inches from the top of the card and 2 inches from the left side (drawing a).

12. Now it's time to bring all of your elements together. Insert the pointed end of the metal brad through the hole in the front panel. (The flat side of the brad will be on the front of the card.)

13. On the back of the front panel, attach the cardstock circle by slipping the prongs of the brad through the hole. Spread the prongs to secure the circle to the front panel.

14. Attach the front panel to the back panel with double-sided tape. Apply the double-sided tape around the perimeter of the back side of the front panel, leaving gaps where the circle sticks out on the sides. This will allow the wheel to spin freely (drawing b).

    Now that your card is assembled, you'll need to put images on the wheel that will appear in the window as the wheel is turned. The easiest way is to make little stickers and apply them through the window. Use fun rubber stamps, clip art, text, or photographs on your stickers, or any combination thereof. This is what makes the project truly special and unique. Have fun with it!

STICKER DIRECTIONS

1. To create stickers with your computer, you will need to print your text or images on Avery White Sticker Project Paper. First, open Microsoft Word and create a new document.

2. If you'd like to make a sheet of image stickers, from the Microsoft Word toolbar choose Insert and then Picture. From the Picture submenu, click From File. The Insert Picture dialog will appear. Find the picture of yourself and your fiancé, or any other photo you wish, on your hard drive and select it.

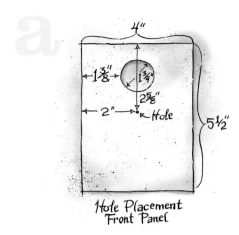

Hole Placement
Front Panel

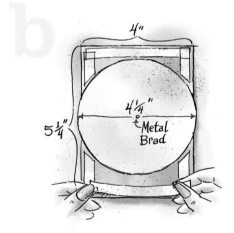

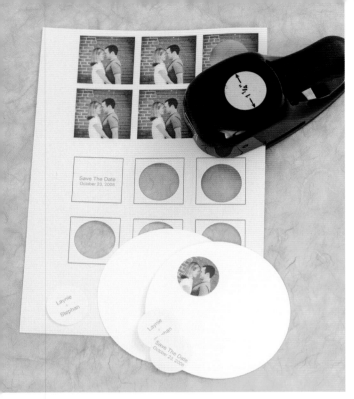

3. Double-click on the picture to bring up the image formatting menu. Click on the Size tab. Size the image close to 1.25 inches by 1.25 inches or a little larger. You'll use a 1¼-inch circle punch to cut out the image a little later.

4. Once the image is sized, copy and paste it several times in the document. Click on the image to highlight it. Hold the Control key and hit the C key to copy the image and then the Control key and the V key to paste the image. Use your mouse to drag and drop your pasted images into rows on the document.

5. When your page is full of images, print it onto the sticker paper.

6. Use the 1¼-inch circle punch to punch out your images.

7. If you'd like to make a sheet of text stickers, from the Microsoft Word Drawing toolbar create a text box. Double-click on the text box to bring up the formatting menu. Click on the Size tab. Size the text box close to 1.25 inches by 1.25 inches or a little larger. From the Colors and Lines tab, change the Fill setting to No Fill and the Line setting to No Line. Click OK. Insert and format your text. Follow steps 4 to 6 above.

8. After you've printed and punched all of your stickers (photo c), adhere them to the wheel through the window. Make sure there are good-sized moves of the wheel between each sticker (photo d).

9. If you'd like, adorn the front of the card with ribbon, rubber stamps, or other embellishments.

Tips & Hints:

- This save-the-date fits into regular invitation-size envelopes.

- Any image or text can be used in the windows, as long as it's formatted to fit within the hole size.

- Any shape of window can be used. There are many fun shapes of paper punches on the market, such as rectangles, scalloped-edged circles and squares, and ovals.

Cost Comparison

Because this type of card is labor-intensive, most invitation shops would charge about $4.50 per card. Our version costs $0.75 each.

Store Cost:	Your Cost:
$4.50	75¢

MR. & MRS. JOSEPH AND CAROLINE WILSON
REQUEST THE PLEASURE OF YOUR COMPANY AT
THE MARRIAGE OF THEIR DAUGHTER

Marianna Elise Wilson

TO

Joshua Michael Taft

SON OF MR. & MRS. KARL AND JULIA TAFT

ON SATURDAY, THE SIXTH OF FEBRUARY

TWO THOUSAND AND EIGHT

AT TWO-THIRTY IN THE AFTERNOON

ST. LOUIS CATHEDRAL
615 PERE ANTOINE ALLEY
NEW ORLEANS

RECEPTION TO FOLLOW

Respondez S'il Vous Plait

PLEASE RESPOND NO LATER THAN JANUARY 12, 2008

NAMES OF ATTENDING GUESTS

WILL ATTEND

COUTURE SILK *Pocketfold Invitation*

I have a soft spot for brides in distress. I was one myself once, so when a frantic bride implored me to help create an invite inspired by a $25 invitation she had seen in a bridal magazine, I was up for the challenge. The set was stunning: a letterpress invitation nestled inside a sewn silk pocket and wrapped with a contrasting satin ribbon threaded through a sparkling rhinestone buckle. The bride couldn't afford couture invitations, but wanted the glam look and to make luxurious silk invitations on a small budget with no sewing.

To help my bride, I created this no-sew version (What can I say? I'm no good at sewing!) that uses inexpensive 12-inch by 12-inch and 8½-inch by 11-inch cardstocks found in nearly every craft and scrapbook retailer around the country. Over the cardstock, I adhered a rich silk dupioni fabric and affixed a satin ribbon with a rhinestone buckle. Dupioni is a beautiful silk with a slightly rough and nubby texture. It's a bit heavier than shantung silk, making it more luxurious and easier to cut and laminate to the cardstock. These invitations can be assembled in minutes and made in any combination of colors and patterns. The best part? This version comes in at under $2.50 per set.

Get Your Craft On:
It's a Girl Thing

Gather your moms and maids together for an afternoon of crafts and bonding. Play chick flicks on the DVD, sip some wine, and let your hair down. No boys allowed!

Supplies Needed
(for one invitation)

For the pocketfold:
- 1 piece of dupioni or shantung silk, 12¼ inches by 12¼ inches
- 1 piece of cardstock, 12 inches by 12 inches

For the invitation:
- 1 piece of cardstock, cut to 4¼ inches by 9¼ inches

For the inclusion pieces:
- 3 pieces of cardstock, cut to 4¼ inches by 6 inches, 4¼ inches by 6½ inches, and 4¼ inches by 7 inches

Other

- Fabric starch spray/spray adhesive
- Iron and ironing board
- Ornate rubber stamp, rotary cutter
- Pigment-based ink pad, black
- ½-inch wide ribbon, cut to 14 inches long
- 1 small rhinestone buckle
- Paper cutter, scissors, ruler
- Computer with Microsoft Word
- Inkjet or laser printer

STATION 1: Fabric
Put your sistas with scissors to the task of cutting, starching, and ironing the fabric.

STATION 2: Pocketfold
Need an easy project for some helpers? Cutting and scoring cardstock is simple and straightforward.

STATION 3: Inclusions
This station isn't for the fraction-phobic. Use your math-friendly friends for cutting the cardstock for the inclusion pieces.

STATION 4: Rubber Stamping
The design divas will love the stamping station! They're in charge of adding ink to paper on the invitation and inclusion cards.

STATION 5: Adhesives
The end is near! For those who don't mind sticky fingers, this station handles the entire adhesive placement on the pocketfold.

STATION 6: Final Assembly and Envelopes
This group brings is it all together. Have them address envelopes, place the enclosures inside the pockets, stuff the invitation packets inside the envelopes, and affix postage. Done!

Don't let the number of steps intimidate you! With a little patience, this project pays off big-time. The invitations are some of the most beautiful and high-end you could possibly make yourself.

DIRECTIONS FOR THE POCKETFOLD

1. From a yard of silk fabric, cut a piece to 12¼ inches by 12¼ inches with your rotary cutter.

2. Lay the fabric piece onto an ironing board or other protected work surface that you can safely iron on.

3. Spray the silk with fabric starch per the manufacturer's directions and then iron the fabric. You want the fabric to be lightly moist, not soaking, with the starch. Too much starch leaves a crusty white residue. Ick! Set the ironed fabric aside.

4. Next, create the pocketfold. It looks a bit difficult at first, but once you make a couple you'll breeze right through the rest. Using the cutting guide, measure and draw the cutting lines onto the 12-inch by 12-inch cardstock.

5. Cut the pocketfold from the cardstock with the paper cutter. Crease and fold as indicated by the dotted lines on the diagram. Smooth the fold lines with the edge of a bone folder to make sharp creases on the cardstock. If you don't have a bone folder handy, use the back of a metal spoon. It works just as well in most cases and you already have several in your kitchen drawers.

6. Now, unfold the cardstock and lay it back-side up on an old newspaper or other protected surface.

7. In a well-ventilated area (outside if you can manage it), spray a fine film of spray adhesive onto the back of the cardstock. Cover

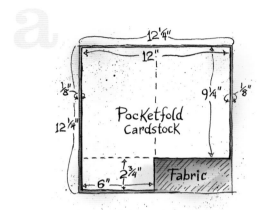

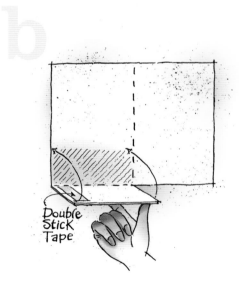

the entire cardstock with adhesive. Let the adhesive set for 1 minute or per the manufacturer's recommendations for a permanent bond.

8. Lay the cardstock, sticky side down, on top of the silk fabric. If you're using a fabric with a distinct pattern or weave, make sure the cardstock and fabric pattern are straight. (This is where the extra ¼ inch of fabric you cut comes in handy. You'll have a little room to make adjustments to correct pattern alignment.) I like to start by setting the fabric down at the top left corner and pressing the fabric down with my free hand as I move my way across and down the cardstock (drawing a).

9. Use the bone folder to press the fabric and cardstock together and create a smooth, firm surface. Let it sit for 1 minute to give the adhesive a little more time to bond. You're almost there! Keep going!

10. Use a rotary cutter to remove the excess fabric around the edges of the cardstock. Rotary cutters will make your life easier. They're a quick way to cut a lot of fabric.

11. Next, you will need to create the pocket that will hold the invitation enclosures. On the lower left side of the pocketfold there is a 2¾-inch flap. Place a line of double-stick tape along the left side of the flap. Fold the flap up and adhere it to the inside of the pocketfold (drawing b).

DIRECTIONS FOR THE INVITATION:

1. Cut a piece of cardstock to 4¼ inches wide by 9¼ inches long.

2. Open Microsoft Word and create a new document. From the File menu, click on Page Setup, and then click on the Paper tab.

Select Custom Page Size from the Paper Size options. Set the custom page size for 4¼ inches wide by 9¼ inches long. Click OK.

3. From the File menu, click on Page Setup, then click on the Margins tab. Set the margin spacing to 0.25 inches for the left and right margins. For the top and bottom, set the margin spacing to 0.50 inches. Insert your invitation wording and then print. The hardest part of this project is deciding on and formatting your invitation wording. For a formal invitation like this one, I like simple and traditional wording with a beautiful script font. An engraver's-type font works well, too. Short on fonts? Head over to www.dafont.com for an abundance of free downloadable fonts.

4. Ink the rubber stamp with the ink pad and press the stamp onto the invitation. You'll be adding it as decoration along the top and bottom borders. Set the invitation aside to dry.

5. Once dry to the touch, apply double-stick tape to the back of the invitation. Affix it inside the pocketfold, on the right-hand side.

DIRECTIONS FOR THE INCLUSIONS:
Next, you will need to create the travel information, map, and response cards (or whatever information you want to include with your invitations) using the cardstock you cut.

1. Create new Word documents for each card you're making. In my example, I've made three enclosure cards and need three separate documents for each one.
   For the travel information, create a new document with the custom page size of 4¼ inches by 7 inches.
   For the map or directions card, create a new document with the custom page size of 4¼ inches by 6½ inches.
   For the response card, create a new document with the custom page size of 4¼ inches by 6 inches.

2. For all documents, set the margin spacing to 0.25 inch for the left and right margins. For the top and bottom, set the margin spacing to 0.50 inch. Insert your wording. Then save your work and print.

3. Rubber stamp each card and set aside to dry. I love rubber stamping! There's really no easier way to put great graphic details onto paper. Stamps can be found online and at craft stores in literally thousands of designs. You're sure to find something that coordinates with your theme. In my example, I used a very ornate border. For a more modern approach, I suggest a bold geometric shape like open circles. A garden-themed invite would be stunning with a large flower stamp like a peony or poppy.

DIRECTIONS FOR THE ASSEMBLY:

1. This part is so easy! Layer the inclusion cards on top of each other from largest to smallest and place into the pocket.

2. Close the pocketfold and wrap the ribbon around it.

3. Take one end of the ribbon and slide it through the rhinestone buckle. Now, take the opposite end and thread it through the buckle from the other direction. The ribbon will overlap. Tuck one end under the buckle and other ribbon. It will be hidden. After all that work, you now have an invitation like no other. Great job!

Tips & Hints

- This invitation fits into regular business-size and #10 policy envelopes.

- You can use any lightweight fabric for this project. Silks and cottons work best.

- Starch fabrics before you cut to help prevent frayed edges.

- Should your fabric start to fray, apply a seam sealant to the edges. (Seam sealant products can be found in nearly every fabric and craft store.)

- If you can, apply the spray adhesive outdoors. At the very least, work in an area with open doors and windows. The fumes can be quite overwhelming when doing a big project.

- To help save on postage costs, use lighter-weight papers for maps, directions, or other inserts. The heavier the overall weight of the invitation, the more postage you'll pay.

- Scrapbook retailers carry cardstock in hundreds of colors and patterns, allowing you to create a unique palette to compliment your wedding theme. Many retailers will offer discounts for bulk purchases of cardstock, and shopping during seasonal sales can help you save even more money.

- Buying fabric online will save you a bundle. Look for great deals near holidays and sign up for companies' mailing lists to be alerted to their upcoming sales.

- Unsure about the quality or color of a fabric you've found online? Many online retailers will send you samples of fabrics so that you can see the quality and weight before you buy.

For a rustic look, try this alternate pocketfold design with faux suede fabric.

Cost Comparison

High-end stationers charge upward of $20 each for very basic silk invitations. The DIY Bride version costs less than $2.50 each to make. That's a savings of more than 90 percent!

Store Cost:	Your Cost:
$20	**$2.50**

Our joy will be more complete if you can share
in the marriage of our daughter

Maya Anusha Prati
to
James Marcus Logan

Son of Lawrence and Karen Logan

On Saturday, the nineteen of September
Two Thousand and Nine
At four o'clock in the afternoon

Los Gatos History Club
123 Los Gatos Boulevard
Los Gatos, California

SAVVY *Stamped Invitations*

Behold the rubber stamp. Oh, sure, it may look like a piece of bumpy red rubber, but it's actually a tiny print shop that can turn a basic, boring invitation into a piece of fine art.

For beginners, rubber stamping is blissfully simple. Basically, you put ink on the raised surface of the stamp and press the inked stamp onto a piece of paper. What could be simpler? If you're an instant-gratification girl like me, you'll love this craft.

All you need to get started is a rubber stamp, ink, and a way to clean your stamp. (I prefer a stamp scrub pad, but you can use baby wipes or even a gentle household cleaner on paper towels.) Pick up stamps and stamps supplies at craft stores, scrapbook shops, and online. For the more adventuresome, have your own design made into a stamp. Check the resources section for a list of custom stamp makers.

Get Your Craft On:

It's a Girl Thing

Gather your moms and maids together for a "crafternoon" tea. You provide the drinks and crafts; have everyone else bring their favorite tea snack (finger sandwiches, scones, and other home-baked goodies).

Supplies Needed

- White cardstock, 8½ inches by 11 inches. Each sheet yields two invitations.
- Dye-based ink pad
- Rubber stamp
- Paper cutter
- Stamp scrub
- Computer with Microsoft Word
- Printer

STATION 1: Cutting Put your girls with an eye for detail at the measuring and cutting station. A perfect cut makes your invitations look professionally done.

STATION 2: Stamping Let everyone join in the stamping fun. Buy a few extra stamps and ink pads so that you can have more than one person in the assembly line. Be sure to have a couple of finished examples on display so everyone can see exactly how you want the design to look.

STATION 3: Final Assembly This group brings it all together. Have them address envelopes, place the enclosures inside the pockets, stuff the invitation packets inside the envelopes, and affix postage.

DIRECTIONS

1. Cut the white cardstock to 5 inches by 7 inches with a paper cutter.

2. Now, the hard part. Create your invitation wording in Microsoft Word. I found coming up with the right wording to be the most tedious part of making my own wedding invitations. Luckily, for you, there are some great little places on the web to find inspiration for your invitation wording. Try www.verseit.com, the forums at kvetch.indiebride.com, and, of course, www.diybride.com.

    OK, on to formatting your text. Open Microsoft Word and create a new document. From the File menu, click on Page Setup, then click on the Paper tab. Select Custom Page Size from the Paper Size options. Set the custom page size for 5 inches wide by 7 inches. Now click on the margins tab and set the margin spacing to 0.25 inch for the left and right margins. For the top margin, set it to 1 inch. For the bottom, set the margin spacing to 0.50 inch. Insert your invitation wording, format, and then print. That wasn't so bad, was it?

3. Print the invitation onto cardstock.

4. Play time! You now get to decorate with rubber stamps. Ink the surface of the rubber stamp with the ink pad. Position the stamp to fit evenly across the top of the invitation. Press the stamp down evenly and firmly but don't rock it back it forth. Lift the stamp straight up. Set the invitation aside to dry. Easy!

luisa
&
kenneth

invite you to share in their happiness
as they exchange marriage vows
and celebrate the beginning
of their lives together

on saturday, the eighteenth of april
two thousand and nine
at three o'clock in the afternoon

san jose museum of art
110 market street
san jose, California

reception to immediately follow

If an ornate invitation's not your style, try a fun mod look instead. Your choices are endless!

Tips & Hints

- One sheet of 8½-inch by 11-inch cardstock yields two invitations. To know how many sheets you'll need, divide the number of invitations you will send by 2.

- Use rubber stamps on a variety of materials, such as paper, wood, fabric, glass, cardboard, and metal to create a theme. Favor boxes, RSVP cards, thank-you notes, programs, and seating cards can all be customized with your stamp.

- If you have trouble squeezing invitation cutting into your busy wedding prep (and between the dress and reception alone, you are busy!), stationery and craft stores offer precut invitation kits.

Cost Comparison

Custom wedding invitations easily cost $2.50 or more. A DIY Bride can make her own invitations for under $0.35 each when made in bulk.

Store Cost:	Your Cost:
$2.50	35¢

CUSTOMIZED MAP *Cards*

Tell your guests where to go—and show them how to get there—with stylish customized map cards.

Having planned many a wedding and soiree, I find it best to assume your guests don't have the navigation skills of Magellan, especially when they're not familiar with the city or venue where your wedding is being held. A simple, clearly drawn map is a thoughtful addition to your invitation package for your direction-challenged guests.

Though a map card may take some time to create, it is a welcome addition to your invitation package. These cards contain a map and directions to your wedding venue and reception and are especially helpful to your out-of-town visitors.

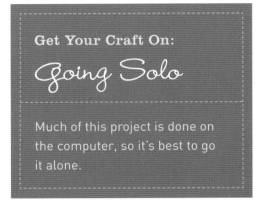

Get Your Craft On:

Going Solo

Much of this project is done on the computer, so it's best to go it alone.

Supplies Needed

- Computer with Microsoft Word and a web browser
- Inkjet or color laser printer
- 1 piece of white (or coordinating color to your invitations) cardstock, cut to 4¼ inches by 5½ inches

My friends, Stefanie and Scott, designed a simple map to get to the church and reception in Seattle without a hitch. They also sent out separate maps highlighting favorite hangout spots, the site of their first kiss, and their dog park. Seeing Seattle through their eyes was a fun way to tour their city.

CARD DIRECTIONS

1. Open your web browser and go to www.maps.google.com or another online map service. Type in the address of your ceremony venue and click Search Maps.

2. A map of the area surrounding your location will appear. Zoom in, using the sliding scale navigation bar on the left side of your screen, until you get a good view of your venue and the nearby major roads and cross streets. You want enough detail to convey exactly where your venue is, but not too many details to confuse your guests. Keep it simple, within a 5 to 10 mile radius.

3. Click the Print icon on the Google™ page. A small window will pop up with a printable version of the map.

4. Right-click on the map and choose Copy from the menu that appears. If you are unable to copy the map, you can take a screen capture to transfer it from the screen to your document. You may also try a different map service, such as www.mapquest.com, www.maps.yahoo.com, or www.mapblast.com.

To capture a screen in Windows, press the Print Screen key on your keyboard, or use a free downloadable screen capture utility such as MWSnap, which is available at www.snapfiles.com. Next, open an image editing program such as Microsoft Paint™ (a standard feature on most PCs). Go to the Edit menu and select Paste. Once the image has been pasted into the editing program, you'll be able to crop the image and edit out any extra objects you don't want on your map.

To capture part of a screen on a Mac, press down on the Command key, the Shift key, and the 4 key at the same time. The cursor will then turn into a cross-hairs icon. Click and drag over an area to select it. When you release the mouse button, the image is taken, and you'll hear a snapshot sound.

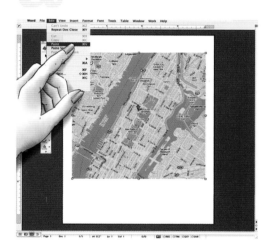

5. Open Microsoft Word. From the Page Setup menu under the File tab, select Custom Page Size from the Settings options. Set the custom page size for 4¼ inches wide by 5½ inches tall.

6. Set the margin spacing to 0.25 inch for all margins, left, right, top, and bottom.

7. Click on the document and paste the map into the document. (Use either the key combination of the Control key and the V key or go to the Word toolbar and click Edit and then Paste Special from the drop-down menu.) (drawing a).

8. Save the document. One of my college professors was notorious for saying, "Save your documents because an unsaved document will never save you." OK, he was a little eccentric, but the advice was solid. Save yourself from the unwanted stress of losing unsaved work to any number of random glitches that are certain to occur after you've just spent hours creating a perfect masterpiece.

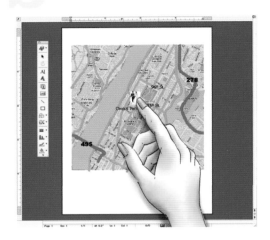

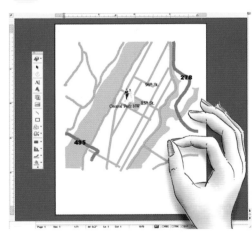

9. Double-click on the map to select it. A black border will appear around the map to indicate it has been selected and the Format Picture dialog box will open.

10. Click on the Layout button and choose In Front of Text for the format.

11. Next, use lines and curves from the drawing toolbar to trace the streets and highways on the map. If your drawing toolbar does not open by default, simple go to View, Toolbars, and click on Drawing to open it. Use the Format Auto Shape menu to cus tomize the look of your lines. You can use dots and dashes as your lines as well as increase or decrease the line thickness to your liking. I prefer using straight, bold lines. They're easier for guests to read while driving.

12. Once the street lines are in place, add labels to the roads. To do so, click on the Text Box button on the Drawing Toolbar. Place your cursor on the location you'd like to create a text box. Click or drag in your document window to create the text box. Now click inside the text box to add the street or location name. You can format the text box by double-clicking on it. A dialog box will appear which allows you to change the background, borders, and other options to cater to your personal style (drawing b).

13. Mark your ceremony location by using a cute icon or graphic. Check out www.clipart.com and resources.bravenet.com/clipart for free and inexpensive graphics.

14. Delete the original map. Simply click on the map and press the Delete key. You should now have only the drawing left on the page (drawing c).

15. Print the map onto your cardstock.

16. Create a new document with a custom size of 4¼ inches by 5½ inches and ¼ inch margins along all sides. Type in and format the written directions to your venue. Print on the back side of the map card.

Tips & Hints

- Simplicity is best when designing your maps. Use as few details as you can to make the map easily read while your guests are traveling to your destination.

- New to Word? There are many great online tutorials for using Microsoft Word. The best ones are done by Microsoft and can be found at their website: www.microsoft.com.

- To create shapes to represent outlines of cities, bodies of water, or points of interest, use the AutoShapes feature in the Drawing toolbar of Microsoft Word.

- Personalize your map by using different fonts, lines, and colors.

Cost Comparison

Custom maps cost about $2 per piece from wedding map designers. A DIY Bride can make these for the price of a half-sheet of cardstock, about $0.10 each.

Store Cost:	Your Cost:
$2	10¢

PEEK-A-BOO *Thank-You*

The wedding's over. You're back from your honeymoon, and you've just gone through the massive mound of great gifts lavished upon you by your nearest and dearest. Piled high are expensive housewares, fistfuls of cash, and unique treasures you didn't even know you wanted.

Being the style maven you certainly are, an ordinary boxed thank-you card just won't do for these lavish gifts. This little gem of a card is not only fun and flirty, but also gives your guests a little thank-you gift: a picture of the bride and groom tucked behind an overlay on the card.

Schedule a dedicated evening with your beloved to cuddle up, pour some wine, and spend some quality time coming up with unique and clever ways to say "thanks" for all of those swell gifts. Remember: Be sincere, be kind, and be yourself. Those are the best thanks anyone can get.

The project is very easy to assemble, but it does take some time to cut and score all of the pieces. Grab some friends and family, pre-wedding, to assemble the cards. Post-wedding, just slip in the pictures and write your thank-you notes inside.

Supplies Needed

- ½ sheet of cardstock (5½ inches by 8½ inches) for the base of the card
- 1 piece of cardstock, cut to 4 inches by 5¼ inches, for the peek-a-boo overlay
- 1 picture of the bride and groom, cropped to 3½ inches by 4¾ inches
- Double-stick tape, ¼ inch wide
- Hole punch, 1/16-inch hole size
- Satin ribbon, ⅛ inch wide
- Pencil
- Ruler or straightedge
- Craft knife
- Bone folder

STATION 1: Creating the Base Assign the cutting and folding of the base pieces to whomever wants the "easy" job.

STATION 2: Overlay Prep Up for more challenging tasks? This group cuts the overlay cardstock to size plus measures and marks the score lines. Set your multitaskers at this station.

STATION 3: Scoring, Cutting, Punching Who needs to get their aggression out? This station is perfect for those that want to score lines in the overlays, slice the "X" in the middle, and punch the holes.

STATION 4: Final Assembly This group brings it all together. They're in charge of attaching the overlays to the bases, inserting the photographs, and tying the ribbon.

DIRECTIONS

1. Fold half the sheet of cardstock in half, along the short side, to create a 4¼-inch by 5½-inch card. Crease the fold with the bone folder.

2. On the inside of the card, start writing a thank-you message to your guest(s). By starting messages in this step, you won't waste a finished card if you make a mistake. The thank-you can be formal or informal, silly or serious, but always be sincere and put a personal message inside. Set aside.

3. On the underside of the 4-inch by 5¼-inch overlay piece, measure in ¼ inch from each side and mark with a pencil (drawing a).

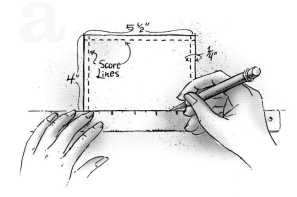

4. Line up the straightedge or ruler with your markings. Using the small pointed tip of your bone folder, score along all four sides (photo b). Fold along the score lines and crease the folds. Unfold.

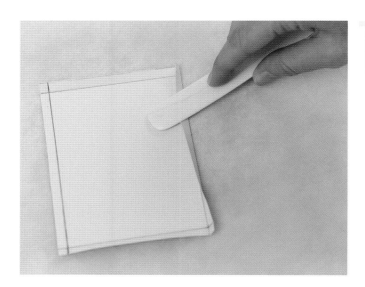

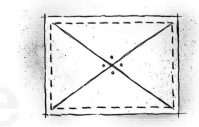

5. Next, make cuts in the center of the overlay. This will open up to reveal your beautiful picture underneath. To do this, lay your straightedge or ruler diagonally across the overlay. Take your craft knife and slice from the inner corner of your fold line on the left to the inner corner on the right. Watch those fingers! Craft knives are notorious (at least in my hands) for slipping, especially when the blade gets dull. Have plenty of new blades (and Band-Aids®) on hand. Now, lay your straightedge across the opposite corners and cut. You'll have cut a big "X" in the middle of your overlay piece (photo c and drawing d).

6. Punch small holes in each of the pointed "flaps" on the overlay. Try to put the holes in roughly the same position on each of the flaps. The symmetry looks nice and helps the ribbon lay flat when you tie it (drawing e).

7. Apply double-stick tape to the edges of your overlay piece and affix it to the front of the card. Make sure it is nicely centered. Use the bone folder to press the affixed piece securely to the bottom card.

8. Open the flaps and insert the photograph. (Aren't you just a vision of newly wedded loveliness?)

9. Thread the ribbon through the punched holes and tie a sweet little bow. Don't be freaked if your bows aren't perfect. Practice, practice, practice until you come up with a system to get yours looking their best. Remember, they're going to get smashed in the envelope, so don't fret too much (photo f).

Tips & Hints

- This thank-you note fits into regular 4⅜ inch by 5¾ inch invitation-size envelopes.

- As an alternative to punching holes and securing the flaps with ribbon, use a wax seal or small label to cover the flap edges.

- Instead of using the same picture in every card, add a snapshot of you and the recipient from the wedding for an extra-personalized thank-you.

- For a fun surprise, write an extra message on the front of the base card before you insert the photograph.

- Cardstock is available in dozens of colors and textures. Have fun playing with different color combinations.

- Bored with cardstock? Try a beautiful Japanese rice paper or translucent vellum as your overlay piece.

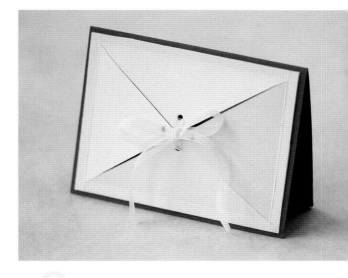

Cost Comparison

Photo thank-you cards from commercial sites cost around $2 each. The DIY Bride version costs about $0.50 each, including the envelope.

Store Cost:	Your Cost:
$2	50¢

2 Beautiful Bride

Elegant Jewelry & Accessories

Every bride gets to play princess on her big day, and what royal would be complete without her baubles and bling? Whether you choose a veil or a tiara, in this chapter I have beautiful projects that will not only save you a lot of money but will also send you gliding down the aisle in style. I also added some wedding accessories for your maids, Mom, and flower girl. The royal entourage is complete!

GLAMOUR GIRL

Bird Cage Veil

You're a modern-day glamour girl with a penchant for fabulously feminine styles from Hollywood's Golden Age. Finding the right accessories to complete your modern-meets-retro bridal ensemble is a challenge. Most bridal salons cater to a more traditional clientele, and authentic vintage accessories are hard to find—not to mention expensive.

What's a girl to do? Why, make her own, of course! Say hello to the birdcage veil. A minimalist alternative to the yards-of-tulle veil found in every bridal shop, the birdcage is 1940s old school Tinsel Town reinterpreted.

Made from a wide, open netting known as either French or Russian netting, this simple veil covers the bride's head only to the eyes. It can be worn over the front of the face, clipped to the back of the head, or worn to the side.

DIRECTIONS

1. Cut a strip of netting 18 inches long.

2. Cut 10 inches of clear thread.

3. With your fingers, weave the thread in and out of the holes in the top row of the netting (drawing a).

4. Gather the netting into the center of the thread (drawing b). Tie the loose ends of the thread together. The top of the veil will be gathered into a bunch and the bottom will be open.

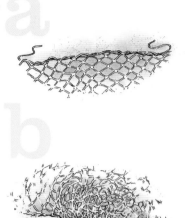

5. Thread the sewing needle with clear thread and sew the gathered part of the veil onto the clear comb (drawing c). Make sure the veil hangs over the front (flat) part of the comb, not the teeth; otherwise it will be backward.

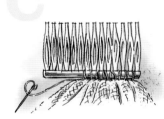

Tips & Hints

- The veil length can be cut shorter if you'd like the bottom edge to fall higher on your face.

- Wear the veil with a feather clip or vintage hat for retro drama.

- Netting is available in white, ivory, and other colors; it can also be colored with regular fabric dyes. Carefully follow the dye manufacturer's directions for best results.

Get Your Craft On:

Going Solo

O solo mio. This is a great project for a quiet afternoon or evening. Grab your drink of choice, put on your "guilty pleasure" music, and enjoy some crafty "me" time.

Supplies Needed

- 1 yard of 9-inch-wide French or Russian veiling
- 1 clear comb
- Scissors
- Clear thread or monofilament line
- Sewing needle

Cost Comparison

Bridal salons charge $60 to $120 (or more) for a birdcage veil. The DIY Bride version costs less than $10.

Store Cost:	Your Cost:
$120	**$10**

VINTAGE NECKLACE *Tiara*

Lizette, a fun and quirky bride I know from collaborating on projects for her vintage-inspired wedding, asked me to create a special project to honor her grandmothers.

I make tiaras from vintage jewelry as a way to use my overflowing stash of flea-market jewelry finds, so together we made a tiara from faux pearl necklaces that once belonged to her grandmothers. With the addition of some new crystals, I turned Lizette's old, broken vintage necklaces into a modern tiara that will become a meaningful heirloom to pass on to her children.

Though Lizette's tiara used vintage pieces, you don't have to. New faux pearls work just as well. Beads and pearls of any shape and size can be used; however, I recommend using sizes under 10 mm to get a nicely proportioned tiara.

Supplies Needed

- 1 gold-tone tiara headband, 8 inches, available at millinery supply shops
- 16—10 mm glass pearls or similar pearls from vintage pieces
- 30—8 mm glass pearls or similar pearls from vintage pieces
- 21—6 mm bicone crystals, tanzanite green, or similar crystals from vintage pieces
- 23—6 mm bicone crystals, crystal, or similar crystals from vintage pieces
- 1 spool 26 gauge gold-tone jewelry wire
- Wire cutters
- Round-nose pliers
- Graph paper
- Felt-tip pen

DIRECTIONS

1. If you're using vintage necklaces or other jewelry for this project, remove the beads and crystals from the jewelry's string or wire. Be sure to inspect the beads for chips, cracks, or other blemishes. Set aside any unwanted pieces. Sort the beads by size, color, and shape.

2. Cut 27 pieces of wire, 3 inches long.

3. On one end of each wire, make a small loop with the round-nose pliers. To do this, grab the very tip of the wire with the tip your round-nose pliers (drawing a). Roll the pliers by twisting your wrist away from you, as far as comfortable (drawing b). Your thumb will change position as the pliers roll the wire into a half a loop. Reposition the pliers back at your starting position, and roll again until you have a completed loop (drawings c and d). Do this for all 27 pieces of wire. It'll take a few tries to find your rhythm, so don't worry if your first pieces seem a bit awkward. Once you get the hang of it, you'll breeze right through this step.

4. Before you begin placing the beads, map out a bead design onto a piece of graph paper. I recommend starting with the tallest pieces, with the most beads, in the center of the tiara and scaling down the number and size of beads as you work toward each end. You'll see that I mix up the shapes and sizes on each wire. I like doing this because it adds that little extra visual element and makes the tiara look like it came from a salon (drawing e on p. 66).

5. If you're copying my design, follow the diagram on the next page to recreate the bead placement on the wires. To create a row of beads, simply place the wire through each bead. Set each beaded wire aside, propped up on a piece of crumpled piece of paper or the edge of a book to keep the beads from sliding off of the wire. I like to make all of my beaded wires at once so that I can see the design develop before they're placed onto the headband.

6. On the inside face of the tiara, mark the center line with a marker. This will help you keep your bead placement balanced as you work. The ink doesn't show when the tiara is finished.

7. Now the fun begins! This step takes you through the assembly process. There are a lot of steps, but it's really just wrapping the ends of the beaded wires around the tiara headband. Beginning with the tallest beaded wire, begin wrapping the wires onto the headband (drawing f on p. 66). Hold the bottom bead against the top rim of the headband with one hand. With your other hand, take the loose wire and wrap it under the headband and then over. Make a couple of tight wraps with the wire around the headband and then cross the wire in front and around the base of the beaded wire. The tail of the beaded wire should end up on the back side of the tiara. The beaded wire should be firmly in place on the headband. There will be leftover wire. Don't cut that yet. I recommend leaving the tails on until you're done affixing all of the wires. If you need to unwrap one of the beaded wires, having the extra wire to grab with your fingers (or pliers) makes it easier.

8. Continue to add each beaded wire until you have them all in place. If you need to adjust their placement, slide them along the band until you are satisfied with their position. When I first started making tiaras, I was really fussy with this step. I spent hours arranging and rearranging the wires until I got it "just right."

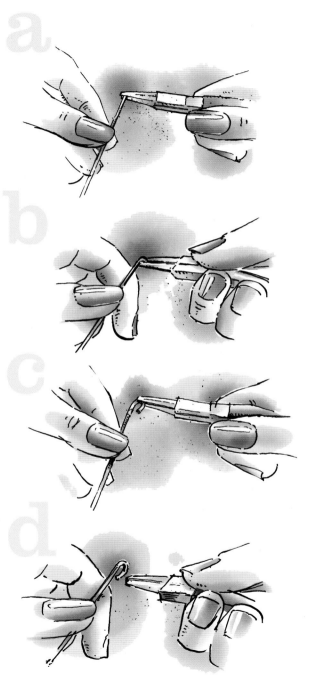

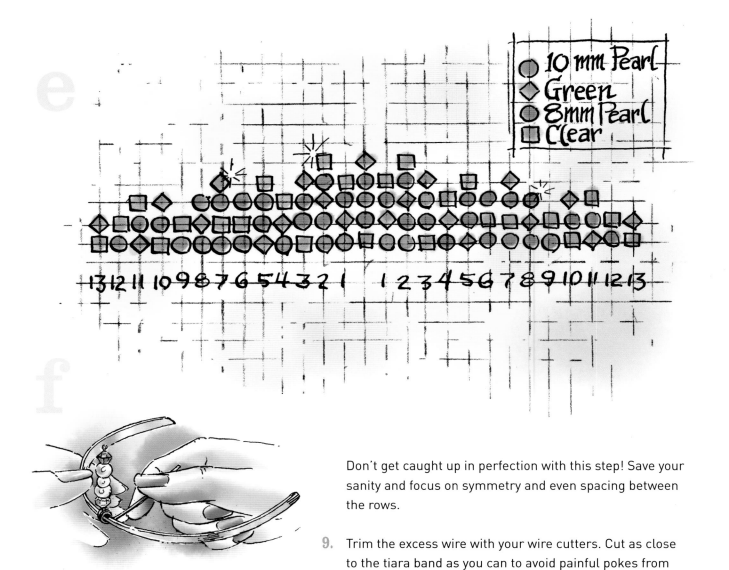

10 mm Pearl
Green
8mm Pearl
Clear

13 12 11 10 9 8 7 6 5 4 3 2 1   1 2 3 4 5 6 7 8 9 10 11 12 13

Don't get caught up in perfection with this step! Save your sanity and focus on symmetry and even spacing between the rows.

9. Trim the excess wire with your wire cutters. Cut as close to the tiara band as you can to avoid painful pokes from the wire. Ouch! Use the pliers to flatten any ends that are sticking out.

10. To finish the tiara, take a length of wire approximately 24 inches long and wind the wire neatly around the band, just before the first beaded wire. Wrap the entire length around the band. This will cover the areas where the wire stems are connected to the headband. It's a nice way to give the tiara a professionally finished look and prevent puncturing your scalp.

Tips & Hints

- Headbands and wire are available in silver or gold tones. They can be found at jewelry stores and millinery shops.

- If you use smaller beads, you'll need larger quantities to fill out a full-size tiara design.

- Beads larger than 10 mm and some vintage beads can be quite heavy. You may need to use a heavier-gauge wire (24 to 22 gauge) to accommodate their weight.

- Use any color crystals or beads. Unusual color combinations are fun and flirty. Try purples and greens or pinks and corals. Clear crystals and pearls are classic and elegant. Red crystals and pearls are daring.

Cost Comparison

Crystal and pearl tiaras cost $250 or more at high-end salons. Our version costs about $30 when using all new materials.

Store Cost:	Your Cost:
$250	$30

FLOWER GIRLY GIRL *Hair Ornament*

You promised your flower girl the opportunity to be a mini princess for the day, complete with a poufy gown and a glittery tiara of her very own.

Because tiaras can be expensive, here's an inexpensive way to create the prettiest, most delicate flower girl hair ornament ever. Creating hair ornaments may seem like a daunting task, but they are actually easy to make. A novice crafter can create a beautiful comb-style tiara using readily available supplies from the local craft store. This version is made of glittered paper flowers, beads, and a wire comb. It's a perfect way to give a young maiden big girl some bling for just a few bucks.

Family Bonding

If your flower girl is old enough, invite her over to help create her very own accessory. Little girls are just made for punching flowers and sprinkling glitter. Save the tough stuff (like wiring and working with sharp tools) for yourself.

Supplies Needed

- Unembellished 4-inch wire hair comb, found at craft stores or millinery shops.
- One sheet of 8½-inch white cardstock
- Flower-shape paper punch
- Jewelry wire, 20 gauge
- Seed beads
- Clear glitter
- Wire cutters
- Small paintbrush
- Large sewing needle, push pin, or nail

DIRECTIONS

1. Punch 12 flowers from cardstock. More or fewer flowers may be needed, depending on the size of the punch and the comb used.

2. Use the paint brush to apply glue to the front of each flower.

3. Sprinkle a generous amount of glitter onto the glue side of the flowers. Shake off the excess glitter. Let the glue dry completely. This can take a while! Take advantage of this downtime and turn your attention to the myriad other projects on your list. Get that seating chart started!

4. With a needle or nail, poke a hole in the center of each flower. Set aside.

5. Cut a 6-inch length of wire from the spool. Fold the wire in half.

6. String 3 seed beads onto the wire, pushing them down to the center (drawing a). Holding the beads in one hand, twist the wires together a few times so they secure the beads firmly in place (drawing b).

7. Thread the ends of the wire into the hole in the flower. The beads will rest in the center of the flower to mimic the stamen of a real flower. Repeat for all of the flowers (drawing c).

8. Starting from the left side of the comb, place a flower on the comb, between teeth, and twist its wire stems around the base to secure the flower in place. Repeat for the remaining flowers until the front of the comb is covered (drawing d).

9. Clip the stray ends of the wires. Add a bit of adhesive around the ends of the wires to help secure the pieces in place and to prevent the wires from poking your flower girl's precious little head. Let dry.

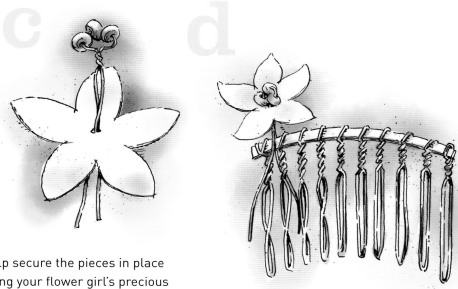

Tips & Hints

- Use different shapes of punches and colors of paper to create a fun, customized tiara. Try punching leaves from brown, rust, and dark green papers for a fall theme. For a vintage feel, try punching flowers from old love letters or pages from a poetry book.

- Craft glitter comes in dozens of colors and can be found at nearly every craft and hobby store.

- To help prevent the flowers from shedding glitter everywhere, spray a light layer of hairspray over the tiara.

Cost Comparison

Flower girl hair accessories can cost upward of $40 in bridal salons. The DIY Bride version costs less than $5 to make.

Store Cost:	Your Cost:
$40	**$5**

RIDICULOUSLY SIMPLE *Drop Earrings*

For this one day, you've tossed aside your love for all things flamboyant and are going for something a little more demure. Instead of your normal outrageous style, try something that gives a nod to the traditional but that doesn't look mass produced. Your mom is sure to approve (but don't tell her about your hot pink and leopard print garter).

A pair of drop earrings would suit the bill, but you've never made jewelry before and your budget is tight. No problem! These bejeweled beauties are a perfect project for a first-time jewelry maker. They can be made with minimal supplies and take about 5 minutes to assemble. Most craft stores carry all the supplies you'll need to get started. If you're not near a retailer or if you're looking for more variety, check out the resources section for a list of great suppliers.

One ambitious DIY Bride created a pair of these earrings for herself. When she discovered how easy they were, she created pairs for her five bridesmaids. With her craft fever in full force, she also made pairs for her mother, mother-in-law, flower girl, and aunts.

Get Your Craft On:

Going Solo

This is a great project to tackle when sitting in front of the TV after a long day at the office.

Supplies Needed

- 2 sterling or surgical steel ear hooks
- 2 headpins, 4 inches in length
- 2 crystal beads
- 2 silver rondelle spacers
- 2 faux pearls
- Wire cutters
- Needle-nose pliers

DIRECTIONS

1. Let's get started! Place one crystal bead and one silver rondelle spacer on the headpin, with the crystal bead on the bottom, then the spacer. Then add one faux pearl (drawing a).

2. With the flat end of the headpin pointing down, hold the wire as close to the beads as possible with the thin end of the needle-nose pliers. Use the pliers to bend the headpin to a 90-degree angle (drawing b). Trim the end of the wire to a length of 7 mm to 10 mm beyond the bend.

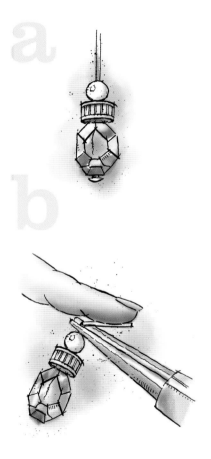

3. Repeat steps 1 and 2 for the second earring.

4. With the edge of the wire squeezed between the needle-nose pliers, turn the pliers half a turn to begin a loop (drawing c).

5. Insert the open loop through the ear hook. Close the loop with the needle-nose pliers.

Tips & Hints

• These earrings can easily be customized by using any combination of bead sizes and colors. If you add more beads or larger-size ones, you may need a longer headpin. Don't be afraid to experiment. Beads are cheap and can be found in most craft stores.

• These make a perfect gift for bridesmaids.

Cost Comparison

Bridal accessories are notoriously expensive. A simple pair of crystal earrings can easily fetch $20 or more in bridal salons. Our DIY Bride version costs less than $1 per pair to make.

Store Cost:	Your Cost:
$20	**$1**

FABRIC FLOWER *Brooch*

I'm not a fan of the traditional corsage. I think it's outdated, over-the-top, and matronly. Today's moms are often youthful, hip, and fashionable. Why not accessorize them with something as fresh and fabulous as they are?

The fabric flower brooch is an easy and elegant alternative to the corsage. Construction is simple. No special tools are needed and the materials are available at most fabric or craft stores—or even in your closet!

Fabric flowers can be made of nearly any fabric or ribbon. Go elegant with a rich velvet or shantung silk,

modern with a geometric print cotton, or shabby chic with vintage-inspired prints.

Do you have salvaged material from your mother's old wedding gown or some aprons from great grandma? This is the perfect opportunity to incorporate heirloom fabrics and buttons.

DIRECTIONS

1. Cut a strip from each fabric, 1 inch wide by 4 inches long, with pinking sheers.

2. Pinch in the center of each strip. (drawing a). Sew through the pinched area two or three times to create a gather (drawing b).

3. Lay the strips on top of each other, crossways, overlapping the gathered centers.

4. Sew through all of the fabric centers to connect them. About 6 to 8 stitches should be sufficient. Push the needle through the fabric slowly—it helps (drawing c).

5. Place a button on top of the flower and sew it into place.

6. Using fabric adhesive, glue the pin back onto the back of the flower. Let dry per package directions.

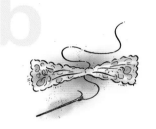

Tips & Hints

- If the fabric feels too flimsy, starch the material with spray starch and then iron. Some fabrics may stain with spray starch. Test a scrap of fabric before you spray the pieces.

- Gorgeous one-of-a-kind vintage buttons can be found at tag sales and on eBay®.

Get Your Craft On:
Going Solo

This flower-power project is best tackled alone.

Supplies Needed

- 4 strips of coordinating fabric, at least 4 inches long
- Pinking sheers, available at fabric stores
- Needle
- Thread
- Button
- Pin back, available at craft stores
- Fabri-Tac® adhesive

Cost Comparison

Fabric flower brooches retail for around $10. A DIY version uses $1.50 worth of materials.

Store Cost:	Your Cost:
$10	**$1.50**

3 Tying the Knot

Crafting Your Wonderful Wedding Ceremony

Your wedding ceremony might be religious or secular or perhaps a mixture of both, but whatever ritual you choose, it should reflect you and your fiancé. Depending on where you get married, personalization can be a tricky thing. Some ceremony spaces will let you deck the space out to your heart's content, whereas others may require you to show some restraint. This chapter has some inspirational to-dos that will make your "I dos" deeply personal, regardless of your venue and their rules. From one-of-a-kind bouquets and boutonnieres to personalized aisle runners and wedding canopies, from flower girl buckets and ring-bearer pillows to pew cones and aisle markers, these touches will make it your own unique wedding ceremony.

BUDS AND BLOSSOMS *Bridal Bag*

Oh, your preoccupation with purses isn't an obsession, really. Sure, the power of the purse compels you to hoard heaps of handbags in your already overfull closets. But that's normal, right? And even though I've heard that your closest pals are staging something called "an intervention," I support your assertion that a girl must have a fab bag for every outfit and every occasion.

So what's this about not carrying a handbag down the aisle with your most glamorous of gowns? Ah, yes, tradition. What if we could turn your favorite fetish item into a not-so-traditional bridal accessory? Say good-bye to boring bouquets and say hello to the Buds and Blossoms Bridal Bag. It's not really a handbag, but a clever purse-shaped bouquet that's sure to turn heads.

Whether you're going for sleek, ornate, bold, or understated, this project can be customized to your unique tastes. Mix and match your favorite flowers and colors to create your ultimate fashion statement.

Made for your Maid

This is a great project to hand off to a crafty friend the day before or morning of the wedding. You'll have plenty to worry about without the added pressure to get one more project done before the ceremony.

Supplies Needed

- 2 blocks of floral foam for fresh flowers, 3 inches by 4 inches by 9 inches (photo a)
- Assortment of flowers, enough to cover the surface of floral foam (order the flowers directly from your florist or buy them yourself from local flower marts or from online growers)
- Floral knife
- Serrated knife
- Stem stripper, for removing leaves and thorns
- Floral wire
- Wire cutters
- Silk ribbon, 3 inches wide
- Twisted satin cord, ⅛ inch wide, available at fabric stores

DIRECTIONS

1. To form the purse's base, wire two blocks of dry floral foam together, creating a single block 8 inches tall by 9 inches long by 3 inches deep. We're using 3-inch by 4-inch by 9-inch floral foam blocks to create a larger block because they're the most widely available at craft stores. Wrap floral wire around the middle of the blocks to hold them together. Twist the ends of the wire to secure them and snip off any excess. A bit of caution here: Wire has a tendency to slice right into the foam. Use a light touch but don't stress if your wire starts embedding itself into the foam. That's normal (drawing b).

2. With the serrated knife, trim the dry foam to shape. The overall size and shape is up to you. Do you have a favorite handbag you'd like to emulate? Or how about a funky shape like a seahorse for a beach wedding? Have a bit of fun with it! Do keep the depth of the foam to no less than 3 inches. This ensures there will be enough solid surface to hold all of the flower stems.

3. After you shape the base, wrap the outer edge of the foam with wire four times, more if you think it needs extra support. This serves two purposes: It stabilizes the foam and it provides a surface to connect the handle to later in the process. (photo c)

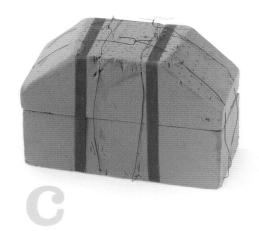

4. Next, soak the foam in a sink or tub. Float the foam on the surface of the water in the sink. It'll sink to the bottom when it has absorbed all of the liquid it can take after about 20 minutes or so. Take advantage of the soak time to start prepping your flowers. Remove the foam from the sink and set it aside on a cookie sheet or in a bowl to catch the excess water. The wet foam will keep your flowers fresh and bright throughout your wedding day.

5. To prepare your flowers, use a stem stripper to remove leaves and thorns. After the stems have been stripped, cut them to a length of about 3 inches. As you're working with the flowers, keep them in water for as long as possible. Have on hand a bucket or container full of water to soak them in between steps. This process takes a while! Allow at least an hour for flower prep.

6. Once all of your flowers are cut, place them into the foam. Insert the stems into the foam starting at the top, working downward.
     I'm going to ask you to think ahead a bit here. If you plan to set your purse on a table later on for display, do not put flowers on the bottom—they'll just get crushed. Instead, cover the bottom with ribbon to conceal the foam. Ribbon can be attached to the

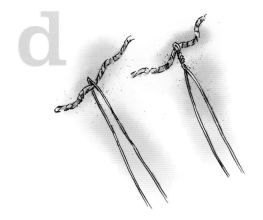

bottom by securing it with floral pins. It's a good idea to do this before you add the flowers to the foam. That way the flowers will conceal the edges of the ribbon. It's a nice finishing touch.

7. You're almost done! The last step is to create and add the handle. Cut two 6-inch pieces of floral wire. Fold each in half. In the center of the wire, place one end of the 12-inch cord. Twist the ends of the wire around the cord a few times (drawing d).

8. Use the free-hanging ends of the wire to secure the cord handle to the wire frame on the foam. Place the wire ends of the cord underneath the wires on the frame where they intersect on either side of the purse (drawing e). Wrap the wire ends of the cord around the frame several times. Warning! The wet foam and flowers can be quite heavy, so make sure your handle is securely in place. Snip off any excess wire.

Tips & Hints:

- Make this project the day of the ceremony to have flowers at their freshest. If you must, this can be made the night before and kept in a foam cooler lined with cold, wet paper towels.

- Go beyond a flowers-only purse. Include berry stems, leaves, and crystal picks for added interest.

- The bag can be preserved after the wedding for a lovely keepsake. Many flowers can be air-dried at home simply by hanging them upside down. Professional flower preservation services are available online and in larger cities if you'd rather leave the extra work to someone else.

- Use silk flowers for this project in lieu of fresh. Substitute Styrofoam® blocks for the wet floral foam.

- Premade handbag handles are available in craft stores to complete the look of a real handbag.

Cost Comparison

Bridal bouquets can easily cost upward of $200. A DIY Bride can make this purse for around $50.

Store Cost:	Your Cost:
$200	$50

BLESSINGS *Bouquet Charms*

When I planned my wedding, I had a difficult time coming up with a way to honor my parents, who had passed away a few years earlier. I wanted something meaningful yet subtle, so as not to detract from the joy of my wedding day. Many of the popular rituals didn't quite feel right, so my fiancé and I decided to include a special blessing in our ceremony programs.

For this project, I wanted to incorporate the blessing as part of the bride's bouquet so that when she walked down the aisle, memories of the couple's loved ones would be close to her heart.

The Blessings Bouquet Charms are a sweet and subtle memorial to a departed friend or family member. One side features a blessing or prayer, the other, a picture of the person to be honored.

Start this project well in advance of your wedding day. The resin takes one full day to dry for each side of the charm. Feeling overwhelmed with scheduling your projects yet? Check out the Project Planning section for help on staying on track with your projects. It's a sanity saver!

Supplies Needed:

- Photographs, 1 inch in size
- Heavy cardstock, 8½ inches by 11 inches, in your choice of background color
- Glossy printer paper
- Computer with Microsoft Word, printer
- Hole punch, standard size
- Scissors, craft knife, photo-safe glue
- EnviroTex Lite® Pour-On High Gloss Resin and Hardener Kit
- Small disposable cup and craft stick
- Paper plate
- Plastic or wood block, smaller than 1 inch wide (to raise the charm so it doesn't stick to the work surface when resin is poured over it)
- Petroleum jelly
- 3 mm flat-back crystals
- Needle-nose pliers, jump rings
- Ribbon, 18 to 20 inches per charm

DIRECTIONS:

1. Cut colored cardstock into 1½-inch squares.

2. Adhere your photographs to the cardstock with photo-safe glue. This creates the base of your charm.

3. In Microsoft Word, create blessings, prayers, or special messages that are meaningful to you, in 1½-inch by 1½-inch text boxes. To create a text box in Word, click on the View menu, open the Drawing toolbar, and click on the Text Box button on the toolbar. With your mouse, click on the document and drag the cursor to create a box. Double-click on the edge of the box to bring up its formatting options. Under Size, change the size to 1.5 inches. Now, click inside the box to type in your text.

4. Print your blessings onto glossy paper. Set them aside to allow the ink to dry thoroughly. Once the ink is dry, cut out the text boxes and set them aside.

5. Punch a hole at the top of the cardstock, about ⅛ inch down from the upper edge.

6. Next, rub a thin layer of petroleum jelly onto the plastic block. It helps prevent the cardstock piece from sticking to the block when the resin begins to cure. Set the block onto a paper plate.

7. Place the cardstock piece with the photo on top of the block, photo side up. Make sure the work surface is level, otherwise you'll have a big blob of resin pooling on one side of your charm.

8. Mix the resin and hardener together according to the manufacturer's instructions. Pour the mix over the cardstock until it just covers the edges. Use the edge of a craft stick to evenly spread the resin over the surface of the charm.

9. Drop the flat-back crystals into the resin about an hour after it begins to harden. Let the charm dry overnight.

10. Re-punch holes in the charm. If there is excess resin on the back of the charm, trim it away with your craft knife.

11. On the back of the charm, adhere the blessings made in step 4 with photo-safe glue.

12. Repeat steps 6 to 10 for the back of the charm, again trimming away any excess resin.

13. Breathe! You're almost finished. Attach the jump ring to the top of the charm and thread the ribbon through the jump ring.

14. Incorporate the charm into your bouquet by tying the ribbon around the bouquet's stems before they are wrapped.

Tips & Hints:

- Use decorative paper punches to create uniquely shaped charms.

- The charms can also be used as fortune tellers in a breakaway bouquet. Include sayings like, "You'll be the next to be married," "You will marry your true love," or "You have a secret admirer."

- After the wedding, the charms can be worn as a necklace, used as an ornament, or included in a scrapbook or shadow box.

Cost Comparison

I haven't seen something like this on the market, so there is no comparison cost. A DIY Bride can make several charms (10 to 20) for around $10.

Store Cost:	Your Cost:
–	$10

HERB *Boutonnieres*

Your guy is all about sleek simplicity. He's masculine and modern and decidedly unfussy. Putting a miniature bouquet of a boutonniere on his lapel just won't do. Forgo flowers and reinterpret the boutonniere for your hip, modern man. Try herbs for an earthy and elegant boutonniere that's both unusual and beautiful.

Herbs also have symbolic meaning. Use basil for love and good wishes. Bay leaves signify glory. Lavender represents devotion. Mint is for warm feelings. Rosemary is for remembrance. Sage bids good health. Thyme lends courage. Mix and match herbs to create a meaningful and fragrant accessory for the guys in your wedding party.

Inexpensive fresh herbs are available in your grocer's produce aisle, and you can assemble them into boutonnieres in just a few minutes.

DIRECTIONS

1. Gather together a few sprigs of herbs. Cut the stems to about 4 inches in length. Strip away the leaves and twigs on the bottom 2 inches of the stems with the stem stripper or use your fingers. Wash your hands well.

2. Hold the herbs together at the stems and wrap them with floral wire from the leafy part of the herb's end to the bottom of the stems (drawing a).

3. Cover the floral wire with floral tape, then cover the tape with ribbon, wrapping from top to bottom (drawing b). Secure the ribbon on the back side of the bundle with a straight pin.

4. Attach the boutonniere to a lapel with the corsage pin.

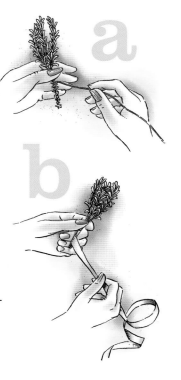

Tips & Hints:

- Keep the completed boutonnieres fresh by placing them in a plastic bag and then placing them in the fridge.

- Use a combination of herbs for added texture and visual interest.

- The best sources for fresh herbs are farmer's markets and organic grocery stores.

Get Your Craft On:
Made for Your Maid

This is a great project to hand off to a crafty friend the morning of the wedding day.

Supplies Needed

- Fresh herbs with stems intact
- Stem stripper
- Floral wire, floral tape
- Wire cutters
- Ribbon
- Scissors
- Pearl-tipped corsage pins
- Small straight pins

Cost Comparison

Florists charge upward of $20 for a simple rose boutonniere. A DIY Bride can make an herb boutonniere for under $3.

Store Cost:	Your Cost:
$20	$3

DECOUPAGE *Flower Girl Bucket*

Your flower girl is under a lot of pressure. Not only does she have to be on her best behavior and work that aisle like a runway model, she's gotta do it with style. Tossing petals "just so" is tough work when all eyes are on you and you're 6 years old. Help your girl out by sending her down the aisle with an adorable flower bucket that's as sweet and girly as she is. She'll feel like a princess, ensuring her best behavior, and you'll save some cash by creating it yourself.

This flower bucket is perfectly scaled for a child and it's an easy project that can be made for under $10. Galvanized buckets can be found at craft shops and garden supply centers for a few dollars. If the shabby chic style isn't your thing, don't fret! This project can be adapted to any theme or color scheme by just changing the paint color and paper selections. Adorable papers are available year-round at craft and scrapbook stores. You'll find an abundance of choices to fit your style and budget.

Get Your Craft On:
Family Bonding

If your flower girl is old enough, invite her over to help her create her own flower bucket. Let her pick out the papers or ribbon. She'll feel extra-special! Save the tough stuff for yourself.

Supplies Needed

- Metal bucket with handle (6 inches to 8 inches tall)
- Acrylic craft paints in the colors of your choice
- Decorative papers in the colors of your choice
- Crepe or tissue paper in the color of your choice
- Ribbon in the color of your choice
- Scissors
- Decoupage adhesive
- Fine grit sandpaper, 150 to 180 grit
- 2 foam brushes, 1 inch to 2 inches wide
- Paper plate or other disposable container

DIRECTIONS

1. Your bucket will need a good scrub with warm soapy water to remove any manufacturing residue. Sand the outside of the bucket. This roughs up the surface of the bucket and helps the paint adhere better. After you're done sanding, use a damp paper towel to remove any residue and dust from the surface of the bucket.

2. Paint it up! Pour some acrylic paint onto a paper plate or other disposable container. Use your foam brush to apply the paint to the outside of the bucket. You'll probably need two or three coats of paint to get a nice, even paint job. Let each coat of paint completely dry before adding the next coat.

3. After the paint is dry, the fun part begins. You get to decorate the bucket! Most buckets have a tapered shape (the top is larger than the bottom) that makes them a bit tricky to cover. Because of the taper, there will be a slight curve on the top and the bottom of the paper when it's cut. Because every bucket has unique dimensions, you'll need to make a template of your bucket's shape. The purpose of the template is to transfer the shape of the bucket to your paper so you know where to make the cuts.

   To get the proper shape, wrap a large piece of scrap paper firmly around the bucket and hold it in place. (Newspaper and scrapbook papers hold up nicely for this task.) With a pencil, trace along the inner-top rim and the bottom edge of the bucket onto the paper. Remember to trace around the raised area where the handles are. Unroll the paper and cut out the shape, extending the length of your template ¼ inch to create a small overlap when the bucket is wrapped. Trace the shape onto the front of your decorative paper and cut it out. For the handles, cut the holes out and cut a slit from the top of the center of the hole to the top of the paper (drawing a). This allows you to just slip the paper over the handles without removing them. It may seem daunting, but don't stress

94

here. This part, even for me, takes some trial and error. Don't expect to get it right on the first try. Be patient and keep trying.

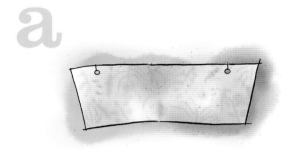

4. To adhere the paper to the bucket, pour some decoupage adhesive onto a paper plate or disposable surface. Dip a clean, dry foam brush into the adhesive and then brush it onto the back of the paper. You'll want to use enough adhesive to get the paper wet, but not saturated. Stick the paper to the bucket and let it air dry.

5. To create that cute little rosette, cut a ½-inch diameter circle from white cardstock. Apply a strip of white glue around the edge of the cardstock circle. Now, cut a strip of crepe paper, about 18 inches long by 1¾ inches wide. This will be the frilly edging of the rosette. Pleat the crepe paper around the circle, pressing it firmly into the glue (drawing b). Continue pleating and adhering the crepe paper until the edge of the circle is completely covered. There will be an open center in the middle of your rosette. Use hot glue to attach a button over the exposed center.

6. For the final touches, wrap a strip of ribbon around the bucket and place the rosette on top of the ribbon. Secure both ribbon and rosette with hot glue for a secure hold. Fill the bucket with petals.

Tips & Hints:

- For a well-worn vintage look, distress the dried finish with sandpaper. To do so, rub a sheet of sandpaper along the rim and on random spots until the metal just shows through.

- Fabric can also be used to cover the bucket. Use spray adhesive or decoupage adhesive to secure the fabric in place.

Cost Comparison

Decorated flower girl baskets cost upward of $25 from wedding retailers. My version costs about $10.

Store Cost:	Your Cost:
$25	**$10**

STEPHANOTIS *Ring Pillow*

Ring pillows are generally pretty darned boring. There's really not much to them. They're square. They're made of fabric. They hold rings. End of story.

As with all my wedding accessories, I want them to be fun, flirtatious, and just a little bit different. As a DIY Bride yourself, you probably want much the same. For this project I opted to create a modern adaptation of the traditional ring pillow, timeless with an unexpected twist.

Instead of fabric, the ring pillow is made of gorgeous, fragrant Stephanotis blooms and a beautiful ribbon. The look is elegant with a touch of whimsy.

After the ceremony the ring pillow serves double duty as a table decoration. The blooms can be preserved and used as part of a scrapbook or shadow box after the wedding day.

One big caveat about using Stephanotis is that they're fragile little flowers. They need to stay in a well-chilled place until the very last minute. Keep them refrigerated before you prep the stems and after they've been placed into the foam.

Get Your Craft On:
Get Your Craft On:
Made for Your Maid

This is a great project to hand off to a crafty friend on your wedding day. She can handle the preparation and care of the flowers while you're basking in your pre-ceremony pampering.

Supplies Needed

- 1 square floral foam, approximately 6 inches long by 6 inches wide by 1 inch tall
- Stephanotis blooms, about 150 to 175 ½-inch blooms
- Corsage or pearl pins, 150 to 175 count
- Ribbon
- Floral shears

DIRECTIONS

1. Soak floral foam until it's fully saturated with water. Set it aside to drain the excess water.

2. Most florists will send Stephanotis blooms with the stems still intact. For this project, we're not using the green stems, so gently pull them off of the white blooms. Stephanotis blooms typically ship with special wired stems that you'll insert on your own later on. (Be sure to ask your florist to ship them with your order!) My floral supplier sent wire stems that had a cylindrical cotton tip on one end that helped keep the blooms hydrated. There are other types of stems and each florist has his or her own preference.

3. After the blooms have been stripped of their natural stem, insert the wire stem into the center of the bloom per the florist's instructions for that particular type of wire stem. There will be plenty of wire stem below the bloom, but you only need 1 inch of it. Cut off the excess with wire shears. Insert the pearl pin into the top of the cotton tip. You're now ready to start decorating the foam (photo a).

4. The next step is to cover the floral foam with Stephanotis blooms. Stick a corsage pin through the center hole in the flower, pushing it firmly into the floral foam. Repeat with the remaining blooms until the entire top, bottom, and sides are covered with blooms (photo b).

5. Wrap a length of ribbon around the covered foam and attach the rings. For my example, I tied the ribbon into a knot on top of the pillow and slid the rings onto the ribbon. The blooms and the width of the ribbon kept the rings in place quite well without the need for tying them in place (untying knots at the altar can be tricky!).

b

Tips & Hints:

- Stephanotis blooms easily bruise and discolor. Take care not to handle them more than necessary before the ceremony.

- Great alternatives to Stephanotis are small roses, Kermit mums, carnations, daisies, dendrobium orchids, and sheets of moss.

- To help keep your blooms fresh, keep them in the refrigerator or a cooler until it's time to use them.

- After the ceremony, the ring pillow can be used as decoration on any of your tables, such as the gift table, the sign-in table, or the head table.

- Stephanotis freeze dry very well. If you're having your bouquet professionally preserved after your wedding, have the service dry your Stephanotis blooms. You can then incorporate them into your bouquet or into a shadow box display.

Cost Comparison

Florists will charge anywhere from $75 to $90 (or more) for a Stephanotis-covered ring pillow. Mine costs just under $45.

Store Cost:	Your Cost:
$90	$45

FAUX METAL *Pew Cone*

Are you embarrassed by the sight of a naked pew? Does an unadorned aisle seat fill you with dread? Are you on a meager budget and do you lack the time to fashion chic décor for your ceremony? Read on, gentle crafter. I have the cure for your decoration ills.

The faux metal pew cone is a quick and easy container to hold flowers, which you can make for about $0.25 each. Yep, that's right: a quarter. (Flowers cost extra.)

Making the pew cones from embossed wallpaper with metallic paint gives the illusion of using vintage tin containers at a fraction of the cost.

While pew cones are pretty common, the metalized paper adds an unexpected and utterly lavish touch to those boring old pews or rental chairs. If you're more of a modern girl or like simpler designs, you're in luck! Embossed wallpapers are available in different patterns and can be painted with any metallic or color of acrylic paint.

Helping hands will make this project a joy. Get a few helpful friends together for cutting and assembling the cones a few weeks before the wedding. On the wedding day, hand this off to your trusted helpers! You'll have plenty to worry about pre-ceremony. Have a couple of people in charge of filling the cones with flowers and another team hanging them. Division of labor makes it go a lot faster.

Supplies Needed

- Embossed, paintable, unpasted wallpaper (available at home-improvement centers and wallpaper stores)
- Hot-glue gun and glue
- Silver or gold spray paint
- Hole punch
- Ribbon or cord for hanging
- Flowers, in water/floral pick (floral picks are available at craft stores or through your florist)

DIRECTIONS

1. Cut strips of wallpaper to 8½ inches tall by 9 inches long. It's OK to make these larger or smaller, depending on the scale of your pews or chairs. If you can, make a few prototypes in various sizes and test them out on your pews a few weeks before the wedding.

2. With the embossed (textured) size facing outward, take one corner and roll the wallpaper, diagonally, toward the opposite corner. This will create a cone shape (drawing a).

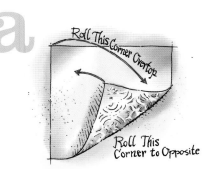

3. Secure the edge with hot glue. Watch your fingers here. Hot glue is, well, hot. It will burn you. Trust me on this one (drawing b).

4. Spray paint the cone with metallic paint. Let it dry. You may need more than one coat. Don't stress. Paint's cheap!

5. Punch a hole into the top of the cone, about 1 inch from the top point.

6. Attach the ribbon or cord to hang the cone on a pew.

7. Insert your flowers. They should be in a water/floral pick to keep the paper cone from getting wet. If the paper gets wet, it'll activate the paste (if the paper is prepasted), causing a sticky mess, or it'll cause the paper to tear under the weight of the flowers. Either situation is a bummer. Avoid it.

8. Hang the cone on a pew. Admire your handiwork. Pat yourself on the back. You did a great job! You may need to adjust the length of the ribbon or the position of the flowers inside the cone to get it to hang right. That's normal. Allow your helpers extra decorating time to attend to any adjustments.

Tips & Hints:

- Embossed wallpaper comes in many patterns. You can find anything from ornate Victorian styles to simple, modern ones.

- Don't overburden your cones with flowers. The holes will rip if the flowers are too heavy.

- Many houses of worship and ceremony venues have strict guidelines about what can be attached to their pews and seating. Check with them before you buy your supplies.

- One standard bolt of wallpaper will yield more than 90 cones.

- If you can, buy unpasted wallpaper. Prepasted paper will become sticky when even the slightest bit wet.

- Buy your wallpaper locally, if it's available. Bolts of wallpaper are quite heavy, which makes them expensive to ship.

- Let your pew cones serve double duty. After the ceremony, hang them on the chairs of the wedding party.

Cost Comparison

Metal pew hangers—without flowers—cost anywhere from $5 to $15, depending on the size. The DIY Bride version costs about $0.25.

Store Cost:	Your Cost:
$15	25¢

HANGING GARDEN *Aisle Markers*

Decorating an outdoor ceremony can be tricky. You want to enhance your space without detracting from its natural charm, but you don't want to spend a bundle on decorations that'll be used only for the few short moments of your ceremony. The solution, my friend, is to make decorations that can be used at the ceremony and then at the reception. You'll save some cash and you'll save some of your precious time, too.

The Hanging Garden Aisle Markers are a beautiful and clever addition to your wedding décor. At the ceremony, these sweet, earthy, gardens-in-a-jar hang from shepherds' hooks along your aisle. Afterward, the wire hangers are removed and the jars serve as the focal point of the centerpieces at the guests' tables.

The materials for these can be found at home and garden centers. The miniature gardens are easy to care for, which means you can make them days (or weeks) in advance.

The shepherd's hooks used here can come in handy after the wedding ceremony. Use them to hang hummingbird feeders, flower baskets, or even lanterns. One bride told me that she uses the hooks every year for the couple's annual 4th of July party. She lines her walkway with the hooks and fills the jars with sand and tea lights. It's not only a lovely way to greet guests, but it's a nice reminder of her wedding day.

Get Your Craft On:
Party Time!

Gather your green-thumbed buddies to pull this project together. These can be assembled a week or so before the wedding, but not much longer if you tend not to be plant-friendly. You'll have enough on your mind without worrying about your horticultural skills!

Supplies Needed

- Shepherd's hook, 4 feet to 5 feet tall
- Clear glass jar, 4½ inches tall by 4 inches in diameter, with a lip near the top
- Silver floral wire
- Wire cutters
- Potting soil
- Pea gravel
- Activated charcoal, available at nurseries or pet shops
- Plants of your choice (some ideas are presented here)
- Scissors
- Spray bottle, water

STATION 1: Washing and Drying
Nothing glamorous here. These fine folks will wash and dry the containers.

STATION 2: Filling Station
Indulge their inner-child cravings for digging in the dirt. Set your pals to filling the jars with rocks and soil.

STATION 3: Planting
The gals with the green thumbs get to put the plants in their place.

DIRECTIONS

1. Wash the glass jar in hot, soapy water. Rinse and dry completely. This sterilizes the jar and helps prevent unsightly and plant-killing mold from growing.

2. Cut a piece of wire an inch or so longer than the circumference of the mouth of the jar. Wrap the wire around the top of the jar, under the lip. Twist the ends of the wire together securely.

3. Next, make the handle (drawing a). Cut a piece of wire 9 inches long. Slip one end under the wire around the lip the jar, about 1 inch in. Twist the loose end to secure it. Repeat on the other side of the jar with the other end of the wire.

4. Place a 1-inch layer of stones on the bottom of the jar. The stones allow water to drain from the soil so the roots won't rot.

5. Add a ½-inch layer of charcoal. Charcoal helps keep the water clean and your plants happy (drawing b).

6. On top of the charcoal, add a 2-inch layer of potting soil (drawing c). Slightly moisten the soil with water from a spray bottle. Damp soil is easier to work with and will allow your plants to hydrate while you work. Don't forget to hydrate yourself, too. Gardening is tough work, even in miniature.

7. Dig small holes in the soil for the roots of your plants. They need room to grow.

8. Remove the plants from their pots and remove the extra soil from the roots. Trim any damaged leaves and branches.

9. While the roots are still moist, place the plants in the holes and pat extra soil over the roots. Make sure the plants are firmly packed into the soil or else they'll fall over.

10. Water the soil until damp but not soaking wet. Too much water will drown the plants.

11. At your ceremony location, insert the shepherd's hook into the ground. Hang the mini-garden on the hook. Remember to hand this job off to someone not in the wedding party. You'll all be busy with pre-ceremony preparations.

12. After the ceremony, place one of the gardens on each guest table. Remove the wire handle by untwisting the ends of the wire.

Tips & Hints

- Enlist the help of four people to set up the shepherd's hooks and terrariums for the final placement at the ceremony. Teams of two make for quick and easy setup.

- Nearly any houseplant will grow inside the mini-gardens. For the best results, use plants that have similar water and light requirements. Good choices are moss and lichens, baby's tears, begonias, spider plants, miniature orchids, small ferns, African violets, and coleuses. Succulents and cacti also work very well.

- Larger or smaller jars can be used. Scale your plants accordingly. If using larger jars, use a heavier, galvanized wire for the handles (available from hardware stores).

- Add more decoration to make tiny gardenscapes. Wood, figurines, sea glass, or decorative rocks add interest.

- The mini-gardens can be made days or weeks in advance if you're good with plants and can keep them thriving that long!

- If creating a mini-garden doesn't suit your fancy or your style, fill the jars with sand and shells, flowers, or candles to fit your décor and theme.

Cost Comparison

Aisle décor from florists can be expensive. Small floral arrangements on shepherd's hooks cost more than $60 each. The DIY Bride hanging gardens cost about $30 each.

Store Cost:	Your Cost:
$60	**$30**

BOOKLET *Program*

At 22, I went to a coworker's wedding, my first wedding experience outside of those in my family circle. It was a lavish, multicultural ceremony with rituals and traditions that were completely new to me and to several of the other invited guests.

There was no information or explanation about what was going on, so I sat in the back with the other outsiders and endured, rather than fully enjoyed, the lengthy ceremony.

The best weddings are those that make the guests feel like they're an important part of the day. They are, after all, there to support you and share their love.

Programs are an easy way to let your guests know what to expect during the ceremony, give them a who's who overview, and offer explanations behind any important or special traditions and symbols. It's an inclusive gesture truly appreciated by those not familiar with your traditions. There are no set rules about what goes into a program. You may include as much or as little information as you think would benefit your guests.

The booklet-style program is fairly easy to make. The booklet is made by folding 8½-inch by 11-inch paper in half and binding the cover and pages together with a ribbon. The only tricky part of the operation is getting the pages arranged properly. Because you'll create 4 pages per sheet of paper (2 pages on front, 2 on back), the pagination takes a little time to work out.

One sheet of paper creates a 4-page booklet. Two sheets of paper create an 8-page booklet. Three sheets of paper create a 12-page booklet (drawings a, b, c on pp. 113–114).

My friend Becky was struck by how important her programs were. "I didn't think our guests would be that interested in our programs but, again and again, we've heard about how much they loved learning about our selection of readings and music and the short bios we included in our program pages. I was touched by that."

Get Your Craft On:

This project works well for small groups. After the programs have been designed and printed, divide your crew into three stations:

Supplies Needed

- Computer with Microsoft Word
- Printer
- 1 sheet of 8½-inch by 11-inch cardstock in the color of your choice
- 1 to 3 sheets of 8½-inch by 11-inch printer paper
- 2 lengths of ¼-inch- or ⅜-inch-wide ribbon, 2½ inches long
- Bone folder
- Mini hole punch

STATION 1: Score and Fold
This group scores and folds the papers and cardstock.

STATION 2: Holes
This group punches holes.

STATION 3: Final Assembly
This group brings it all together and assembles the pieces.

DIRECTIONS

1. Open Microsoft Word and create a new document.

2. Go to File, Page Setup, and select Landscape under Orientation. Click OK.

3. On the File menu, click Page Setup, and then click the Margins tab. In the Multiple pages list, select Mirror Margins, then set the top and bottom margins to 0.50 inch, the inside and outside margins to 0.75 inch, and the gutter to 5.50 inches. This will give you one page per sheet on the screen, alternating from right (the odd pages) to left (the even pages).

4. Enter your program text and pictures sequentially from page 1 to the end. Format the text size, fonts, and colors to your liking. A typical 4-page program will follow this layout:

PAGE 1: TITLE PAGE
The names of the bride and groom, with the wedding date and the location on this page.

PAGE 2: THE WEDDING PARTY
This page is used to introduce the parents of the bride and groom, the bridal party, the attendants, and the ceremony officiant.

PAGE 3: THE CEREMONY EVENTS
The order of events is presented here. Detail each event, such as the seating of the mothers, the processional, the exchange of vows, readings, music interludes, and the recessional. Explain any cultural or religious traditions that may be unfamiliar to your guests.

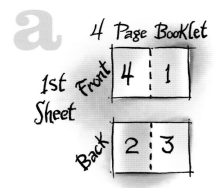

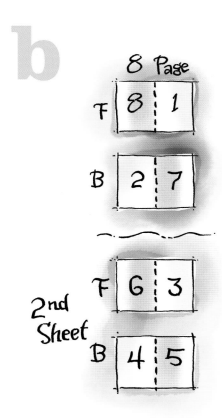

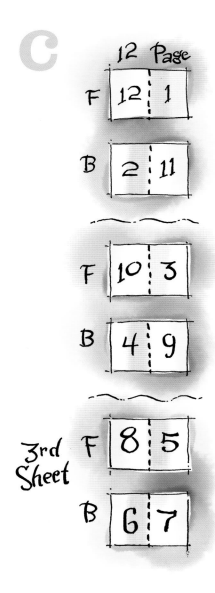

PAGE 4: THE DEDICATION AND THANK-YOU
This space is used for honoring any deceased loved ones and for thanking family and friends for their support.
Save the document.

5. Print the odd pages of your document by selecting Odd Pages from the Print menu at the bottom of your Print dialog box.

6. After the odd pages have printed, return to the Print dialog box and select Even Pages. Click the Options button in the Print dialog box and check the Reverse Print Order box.

7. Now feed the odd pages back through the printer to have the second page printed. Check the user's manual for specifics on which way to feed the paper into the printer.

8. Score the pages and the cover cardstock down the center with the tip of the bone folder. Crease the fold with the smooth side of the bone folder for a nice, crisp finish.

9. Insert the pages inside the cover, stacking them on top of each other.

10. Punch holes in the cover and in the pages, 1 inch from the top, 1 inch from the bottom, and ½ inch from the edge.

11. Align the holes and close the booklet. Insert ribbon into the holes and tie into little bows or simply into knots. Trim off any excess, if you'd like, or leave the extra ribbon as decoration.

Tips & Hints

- Any type of paper can be used for the cover. Japanese washi paper, color scrapbook paper, translucent vellum, lace paper, even starched fabrics look wonderful as program covers.

- Not sure how to decorate the cover? Affix a printed label, rubber stamp your monograms, or add a picture of you and your fiancé.

- Don't be afraid to play around with different binding materials. Ribbon is always elegant, of course, but you could easily use raffia or twine for a rustic look. Small twigs are delightful. Chopsticks are fun and unusual when woven through the punched holes. No ribbon needed!

- Fun ideas and helpful information to include in your program are special notes to your guests, the relationship of any wedding party member to the bride or groom, the significance of the wedding date or location, a note about the music performed, or the story of how you met.

Cost Comparison

Custom-designed programs start at $2.50 each. A DIY Bride can make her own for about $0.50 each.

Store Cost:	Your Cost:
$2.50	50¢

Matron of Honor
Mary Gagnon

Bridesmaids
Beth McGarrigle
Cheryl Ashby

Flower Girl
Amanda Gagnon

Best Man
Roy Wilson

Groomsmen
Gary Coleman
Emil Valliar

Ring Bearer
James Hitchcock

KERRY & KEVIN

PRELUDE

SOLO
There is Love

LIGHTING OF CANDLES

SEATING OF MOTHERS

PROCESSIONAL
Canon in D

INVOCATION

MARRIAGE VOWS

EXCHANGE OF RINGS

PRESENTATION OF
THE BRIDE & GROOM

RECESSIONAL

PERSONALIZED PROGRAM *Fan*

The problem with having an outdoor wedding is, well, it's outdoors. Summertime ceremonies can get terribly warm, especially for your guests, as they swelter under the afternoon sun before and during your nuptials.

Help your guests keep their cool with beautiful hand-held fans that double as programs. They're a cinch to make and downright practical, too.

Although there are no set rules about what your program must contain, some basic information about the ceremony helps your guests follow along and feel included.

I suggest including the following:

- An outline of the wedding ceremony and the order of events
- The names of the wedding party members and their relationships to the bride and groom
- An explanation of any religious or cultural traditions and rituals
- The names of any musicians and readers you may have
- Any special messages or thanks you'd like to share. The fan shape is created by scanning the fan template on page 121, or one of your own, onto your computer. Insert the scanned image into a Microsoft Word document and add your own words and artwork. Print, cut, and embellish. Voila!

Get Your Craft On:
It's a Girl Thing

Gather your moms and maids together for an afternoon of crafts and bonding. This is a BYOS party: Bring Your Own Scissors! Having everyone supply their own tools not only saves you some cash but makes for fun invitation wording. Print out the fan pages the day before your crafting soiree so they're ready to go on assembly day.

Supplies Needed

- Cardstock, 8½ inches by 11 inches, in the color of your choice
- Scissors
- Computer with Microsoft Word
- Scanner
- Inkjet or laser printer
- Rubber stamps
- Ribbon or other embellishments (optional)

STATION 1: Cutting
Set everyone to cutting out the fan blades. Many hands make light work. Do make sure they keep the blades in order! Hand out a prize for the person who cuts the most blades.

STATION 2: Rubber Stamping
Save this step for your artsy helpers. Although stamping isn't hard, this step is perfect for anyone with a keen eye for detail.

STATION 3: Embellishing
Get everyone involved in adding ribbon or embellishments to finish up the project.

DIRECTIONS

1. Scan the fan template into your computer. Check the user's manual for specifics on how to scan for your brand and model of scanner. Save the image to your desktop.

2. Open Microsoft Word and create a new document.

3. Under the File menu, go to Page Setup. Set the Orientation to Landscape.

4. From the File menu, select Page Setup. Set the top margin to 0.45 inch, the bottom margin to 0.40 inch, and the left and right margins to 0.75 inch.

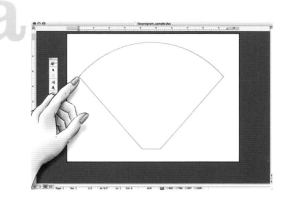

5. Under the Insert menu, go to Picture and then From File. Find the scanned fan template and select it.

6. The template will now appear in the center of the document. You'll probably need to resize the image to fit your page. You can do so by simply clicking on the image to highlight and dragging one of the corners or sides.

7. Next, insert wording for your program on top of the template. This is the fun part! You can create any design you want and use whatever wording that expresses what you and your sweetie want to convey to your guests. This part of the project is a swell opportunity for you to collaborate! To insert the wording, you'll need create text boxes (drawing a). Create a text box by going to the Drawing toolbar and click on the Text Box button.

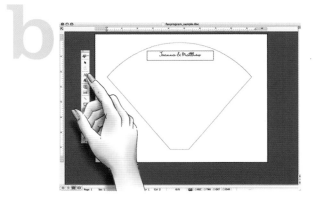

8. With your mouse, click onto the area of the template where you'd like to insert text and drag your cursor to create a box. Click inside the box and type in your text. Don't be afraid to play around with different fonts and font sizes! Add color or bold elements for even more pizzazz. Because the template is a nonstandard shape, you may need to create several text boxes to fit your wording inside the template (drawing b). You can move and resize the text boxes as needed with the mouse.

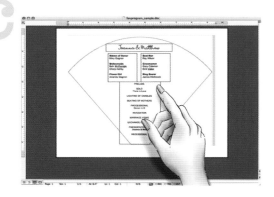

9. After you have inserted your text, format the text boxes to remove their borders (drawing c). Double-click on a text

What you put on your program fan is what makes the ceremony unique to you. Play around with different words and designs to come up with your perfect program.

box and its formatting palette will appear. Under Fill select No Fill and under Line select No Line (by selecting No Fill the text boxes will be transparent. That will allow you to overlap them if necessary without covering up text in other boxes).

10. Save your document and print it onto cardstock.

11. The back side of the fan can be printed as well, but do this before you cut out the shape! Flip the paper over and use a new document to create a second template for the back. Insert the couple's picture, a monogram, or a special poem or quote. Save the document and print it onto cardstock, making sure the back side prints in the same orientation as the front.

12. Cut out the fan shape, just inside the lines, with a pair of sharp scissors. Add ribbon or other embellishments if you'd like. An inexpensive wood handle or craft stick (available at craft stores) will turn your program into a paddle fan.

Tips & Hints

- You can use any shape for the fan. Simply use a piece of clip art, draw a design, or trace the outline of a fan you like onto scrap paper, then scan.

- Embellish the fan by punching a hole near the bottom and threading ribbon through. Adding a rubber-stamped image or affixing flat-back crystals is a great way to add dramatic touches.

- Instead of printing on both sides of the fan, laminate a sheet of coordinating cardstock or fabric on the back. Coat the back side with spray adhesive, then attach the cardstock or fabric. Cut the fan shape from the laminated pieces and set the fan aside to completely dry.

Cost Comparison

Custom fan programs cost anywhere from $1.50 to $5 each from stationers. The DIY Bride version costs about $0.30 each when made in bulk.

Store Cost:	Your Cost:
$5	30¢

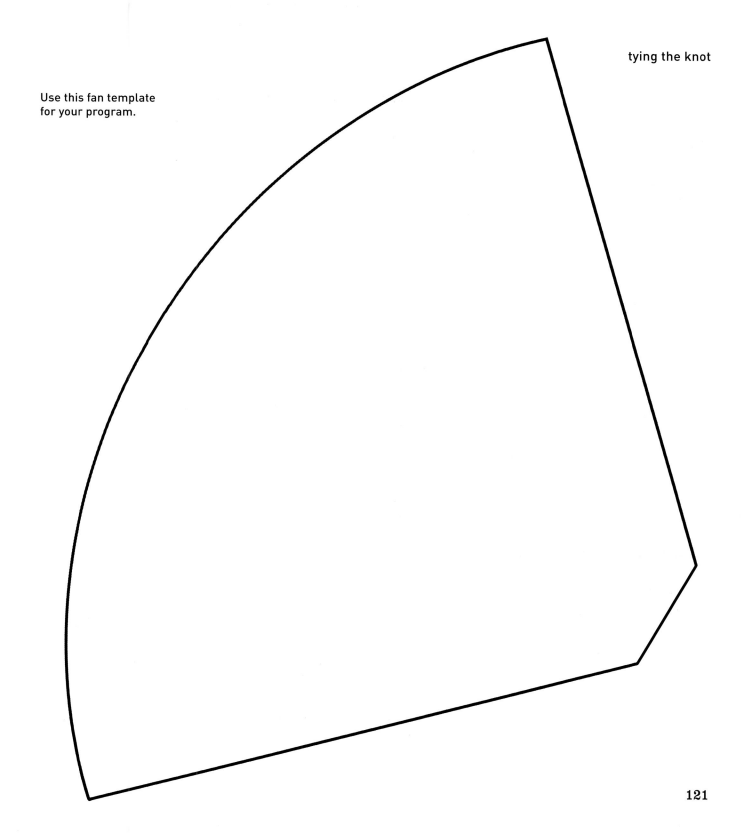

tying the knot

Use this fan template
for your program.

"BEST DOG" *Collar*

When it came time to ask your nearest and dearest to be part of your wedding party, he was on the top of your list. You couldn't imagine your wedding day without him, even though his participation raises some eyebrows from certain relatives. Sure, he's a little hairy and his table manners are a bit crude. But, hey, no pooch is perfect.

Including your canine cutie as part of your wedding party isn't as far-fetched as it may seem. Many couples are opting to share the big day with their doggy pals, even having them serve human roles like groomsmen, flower girls, and ring bearers. Send your Fido down the aisle in style with a custom collar, embellished with rhinestones for that extra bit of sparkle.

This project uses a plain, premade nylon collar from your local pet shop as the base. These types of collars are inexpensive and very well made, an important consideration for the dog's safety and comfort during the big day. One big plus: This is a no-stitch option for the sewing challenged.

Supplies Needed

- Unembellished nylon dog collar to fit your dog
- Satin ribbon the same width and length as your dog collar
- Flat-back rhinestones, 5ss to 10ss in size
- Gem-Tac® rhinestone glue
- Flexible fabric glue
- Tweezers
- Upholstery needle
- Toothpick or bamboo skewer

DIRECTIONS

1. Apply a thin layer of fabric glue onto the outward-facing side of the collar (drawing a).

2. Lay the satin ribbon over the glue and smooth it down with your finger, a spatula, or a disposable wooden craft stick to remove any air bubbles. Allow glue to dry completely. Caution! Work in a well-ventilated area. Inhaling glue for long periods of time isn't a good idea (drawing b).

3. Draw the wording or design for the collar onto a piece of scrap paper the same size as the collar. I used "Best Dog," but you could use anything that fits on the collar. How about your pet's name? Or maybe "I Do!"? Place your stones on the design to determine the spacing and number you'll need (drawing c).

4. Use a pencil to draw the design on the ribbon if you're not comfortable placing the stones on the finished collar freehand. Practice picking up the stones and placing them down on the ribbon before you glue them in place to get a feel for the process. Small stones can sometimes be a bit uncooperative. I've sent many flying across the room with my tweezers (drawing d).

5. Pour a quarter-size amount of Gem-Tac glue onto a piece of paper.

6. Dip the toothpick or bamboo skewer into the glue and dab the glue onto the satin ribbon, a few dots at a time. (No more than two or three at once; the glue dries very quickly.)

7. Using the tweezers, pick up a rhinestone, top-side up, and gently place it onto the glue. Move to the next drop of glue. Repeat steps 6 and 7 until the design is complete (drawing e).

8. Allow the rhinestones to set 2 to 4 hours to completely dry.

9. On the back side of the collar, poke holes with an upholstery needle through the ribbon where it covers the collar's original holes for the buckle latch. Grab your pooch and take the collar for a test run. Remember to tell her how beautiful she looks.

Tips & Hints

- Rhinestones don't stick very well to a bare nylon collar. A leather or cloth collar can be used with or without the ribbon overlay.

- Other types of ribbon can be used: velvet, silk, cotton. You can use strips of fabric, too.

- Flat-back rhinestones are available in a rainbow of colors. Choose shades that coordinate with your wedding colors or that compliment Fido's fur coat.

- You can create nearly any design you'd like. Embellish with the dog's name, a custom wedding logo, or even a meaningful saying.

Cost Comparison

Custom bejeweled dog collars cost around $50. The DIY Bride can make her own for under $15 for a small to medium-size dog.

Store Cost:	Your Cost:
$50	$15

PERSONALIZED *Aisle Runner*

When I think of aisle runners, high fashion doesn't exactly come to mind. I know their purpose is to protect the gown and shoes you just spent a small fortune on, and don't get me wrong—I'm a fan of practicality. I just like it served with a side of style.

It doesn't take much money or effort to transform a simple white aisle runner into a work of art. All you need is a paper aisle runner, some acrylic craft paint, a couple of paint brushes, and a template.

Before you make this project, check with your venue about their aisle runner policies. Some have strict rules about the length and material you can use; others completely prohibit aisle runners.

Supplies Needed

- White paper aisle runner, 36 inches wide by 50 feet to 150 feet long, depending on the length of your aisle, available at craft and party supply stores.
- Pencil for tracing
- Acrylic craft paint in the colors of your choice
- Craft paint brushes in assorted sizes, up to a bristle size of 1 inch wide
- Computer with Microsoft Word
- Printer
- Repositionable painter's tape

DIRECTIONS

1. In Microsoft Word, create a monogram, saying, or design you'd like to put on your aisle runner. Be creative! Be adventuresome! This is an excellent place to make a statement about your personal style. Use a favorite movie quote or song lyric. Tie the design in with your invitations and stationery by using a motif such as a leaf or flower. Do you have a talented artist in your inner circle? Ask her to create a special graphic. Monograms are great, too, but beware! Etiquette suggests that the couple shouldn't use the groom's last initial (if she's taking his name, of course) until the ceremony is over.

    Print the design on regular white printer paper. It's best to create your design in black and white.

2. The next step requires a trip to your local copy center. Have them enlarge your print to fit onto a 30-inch-wide surface. This will serve as your template.

3. Trace the design from the template onto the aisle runner (photo a). Slip your template underneath the paper aisle runner into the desired position. Secure it in place with painter's tape. Step back every few minutes to look at the design and make sure the template hasn't slipped. It's easier to make adjustments in this stage than when you're painting (photo b).

4. After your design has been traced onto the surface of the aisle runner, fill it in with acrylic craft paint. Be sure to cover your work surface with newspaper or kraft paper to protect your table or floor.

5. Let the paint dry completely before rolling the aisle runner up.

a

b

Tips & Hints

- Leave the final placement at the ceremony to your groomsmen, location staff, or wedding coordinator, if you can.

- Aisle runners are available at most craft stores, party supply stores, and floral supply outlets.

- Two common types of runners are paper and plastic. *Always* select the paper version.

Cost Comparison

Custom aisle runners cost upward of $200. A DIY Bride can make hers for under $50.

Store Cost:	Your Cost:
$200	**$50**

CEREMONY *Canopy*

The first time I went to an interfaith ceremony I fell deeply, madly in love . . . with a piece of the ceremony décor. It's silly, I know, but my love affair with the chuppah or ceremony canopy has lasted for years. There's something about it that makes any ceremony seem intimate and cozy. To create one thrills me not only because it is pretty to look at, but also because the chuppah symbolizes the home the couple will build together.

If you'd rather not use this project as a chuppah at the ceremony, that's OK. It can easily serve as a canopy over the cake table or any other area at the ceremony or reception.

This is an easy project to customize to your wedding décor. The fabric can be anything you'd like: a quilt from your grandma, lace from your mother's and future mother-in-law's gowns, off-the-rack curtains from a department store, or any other material that suits your fancy.

Get Your Craft On:
Where the Boys Are

Although the canopy is easy to make by yourself, you'll need some handy helpers on the day-of to assemble the altar. Enlist the help of those hunky grooms-men to carry the gravel to the ceremony site, and have some trusted friends put everything together. You'll need at least two people to wrap the poles, fill the buckets, and pull the project together.

Supplies Needed

- 4—2-inch-diameter bamboo poles, cut to 8 feet to 9 feet long
- 4 yards of fabric, 45 inches wide
- Ribbon
- Scissors, handsaw
- Galvanized metal flower buckets or terracotta flower pots
- 2—½-cubic foot bags of pea gravel
- 2—½-cubic-foot bags of sand
- Coordinating needle and thread
- Tulle (optional)
- 8 strong rubber bands

DIRECTIONS

1. Cut the bamboo poles to 8 feet to 9 feet long. (Tip: Many home-improvement and garden centers will cut the poles for you for a nominal fee.) Do not wait to do this on the day of the ceremony!

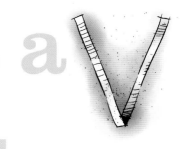

2. To secure the canopy to the poles, you'll need to create some ties. Cut four pieces of ribbon, 14 inches long. Fold each in half and spread them out into a "V" shape (drawing a).

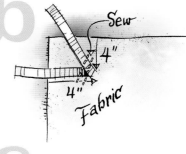

3. Place fabric on the floor and sew the center of the ribbon, at the fold, securely to the corners of the fabric, with about three rows of stitches, about 4 inches from each edge (drawings b and c).

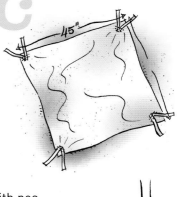

4. At the ceremony location, set the buckets on the ground. Place one of the bamboo poles inside a bucket, in the center. Enlist a helper to hold the pole straight. Pour sand into the bucket until it is halfway full, then fill the rest with pea gravel until it's full and the pole is able to stand erect and upright on its own. Do this for all four poles (drawing d).

5. If you are wrapping the poles in tulle or greenery, wrap them now (drawings e and f).

6. Attach the canopy to the poles by tying the ribbons around the poles (drawing g). If you're using fabric that's on the heavy side, have some clear push pins handy to help secure the fabric to the poles.

Tips & Hints:

- If you don't have access to bamboo poles, closet dowels, PVC pipe, and copper tubing also work well. They can all be found at most home-improvement stores.

- Instead of—or in addition to—tulle fabric, the poles can be covered in real or faux greenery. Placing battery-operated twinkle lights underneath the tulle is quite pretty in a darkened room.

- Great fabric choices for canopies are lightweight cotton canvas, silk, and tulle. My version is a sheer curtain.

- After the ceremony, the canopy can be placed over the cake or drinks table to keep it shielded from the elements.

- After the wedding, use the canopy in your backyard for shade. Or disassemble it and use the pieces for home or garden décor.

Rubber Band to hold Tulle

Rubber Band

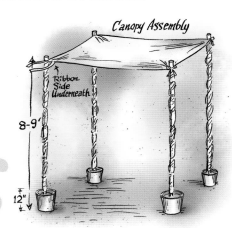

Canopy Assembly

Ribbon Side Underneath

8-9'

12"

Cost Comparison

Custom canopies cost $300 or more; rentals can cost $100 a day. Our version costs about $75.

Store Cost:	Your Cost:
$300	**$75**

4 Having a Ball
The Touches That Make the Reception

You did it! After all those months of planning, you and your fiancé are finally newlyweds. Now it's party time! This chapter shows you how to pamper your guests with high style on any budget. Check out our ideas for decorating those ho-hum rented tables with center-pieces that range from sophisticated to rustic. Guide your guests to their seats with swell seating charts, table numbers, and escort cards. Dazzle your friends and family with glammed-up goodies bedecked with some sweet crystal and rhinestone bling.

RHINESTONE *Monogram Cake Topper*

To say I have an obsession with bright, sparkly things is, well, an understatement. My penchant for affixing Swarovski® crystals to many an inanimate object is legendary in my social circle. An ever-growing collection of bejeweled cell-phone covers, cigar purses, and iPod™ cases is the source of great envy among my glamour girl pals.

Weddings are the perfect occasion for over-the-top glam because they provide me with the perfect candidate for a bit o' glitzy goodness—the cake topper. Although the cost of Swarovski crystals can be a little high, trust me, your one-of-a-kind cake topper will be so cute your cake will be jealous.

For you novice crafters, this project is a bit more complex than most. It requires basic soldering skills and a few days' time to allow the rhinestone adhesive to completely dry. But don't let that scare you away! Grab some extra wire and give yourself some time to practice your soldering skills before you commit to making the final design. It usually takes a few tries to get the hang of it.

Supplies Needed

- Flat-back crystal rhinestones in the color of your choice, sizes 16ss to 34ss
- Stainless steel wire, 1-yard to 15-yard roll, 20 gauge
- Rhinestone or jewelry adhesive
- Wire cutters
- Round-nose pliers
- Hammer
- Tweezers
- 4-inch printout of the couple's monogram
- Soldering iron
- Lead-free solder
- Flux, a paste that helps the solder stick to the metal being bonded together
- Wax paper

DIRECTIONS

1. One of the fun things about this project is that the monogram can be any font or size you'd like. Play around with your font selection, or download new fonts from www.dafont.com to find something that fits your wedding's formality or theme. I recommend having your monogram between 3 inches and 5 inches tall. Anything larger looks out of place on a standard 4-inch to 8-inch wedding cake top layer.

   Let's begin! Using a printout of the couple's monogram as a guide, bend a length of stainless steel wire to the shape of the letter.

   To create smooth curves and twists in your wire, use round-nose pliers to help mold it to shape. However, you'll probably find your fingers are the best tool here.

   Many letters will require only one piece of wire; others may take two or three pieces depending on how intricate the design is. If your letter uses more than one piece of wire, the easiest way to join the wire pieces is to solder them together at the connection points. Don't freak out about soldering! It's just melting pieces of metal together. It does take some practice to get it smooth and even, so set some time aside to practice and get a feel for the process. If you're still not convinced you can do it, super glue works in a pinch but won't likely create a permanent bond between your metal pieces (for recommended soldering points for a simple script alphabet see drawing a).

2. Once your letter has been formed, the next step is to create a way for it to stand upright on your cake. The easiest way I found to do this was to create a V-shaped pick out of the 20-gauge wire and solder it to the bottom of the letter. This pick will slip directly into the cake. On some letters a V-shaped pick doesn't quite work. Extending the length of the wire or adding a straight piece of wire works well on simple shapes like a "T" or "V" (drawing b).

3. To prepare the monogram for the rhinestones, set it on a hard, flat surface and hammer the entire shape several times. Flip it over and hammer on the opposite side. This flattens the round wire so that the rhinestones will better adhere to it.

4. Next, spread a sheet of wax paper on your work surface and pour a small puddle of adhesive onto a corner of the wax paper. (Note: When using jewelry adhesives, work in a well-ventilated area.)

5. Lay the wire form flat on the wax paper. Use tweezers to pick up a rhinestone, dip the flat side of the rhinestone into adhesive, and apply the rhinestone directly to the wire. Hold the stone in place for a few seconds and then move on to the next stone. Complete one side of the monogram and let the adhesive dry per the package directions (usually a full 24 hours). Turn the monogram over and adhere stones to the back of the wire, matching the stones up with the first ones applied. Let the adhesive dry. Once the adhesive is dry, the monogram is ready to use on your cake.

Tips & Hints:

• Acrylic rhinestones are considerably less expensive than crystal rhinestones. Acrylic stones are available in limited colors and don't sparkle as brilliantly as their crystal counterparts but they're less than half the price.

• Use multiple letters in various sizes and solder them together as a fun alternative to using only a single initial.

• Shapes such as hearts, stars, and curlicues are easy to make and would be great alternatives to using initials.

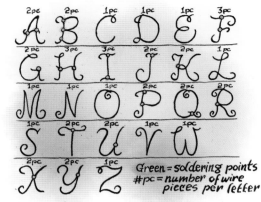

Green = soldering points
#pc = number of wire pieces per letter

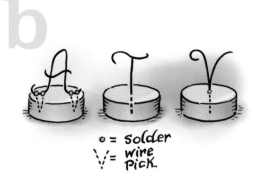

o = solder
V = wire pick

Cost Comparison

Custom wire and rhinestone toppers cost $175 or more. This version costs about $55.

Store Cost:	Your Cost:
$175+	$55

CUPCAKE *Tower*

Ah, the ubiquitous cupcake. When my husband and I served cupcakes in lieu of a traditional wedding cake at our 2000 reception, we were cutting-edge.

Gourmet cupcake shops hadn't hit the mainstream yet, and the cupcake-as-wedding-cake was very much a novelty. Today it's not uncommon to find cupcakes at receptions, and, really, who can resist such a tasty little portable treat?

With cupcakes comes the dilemma of how to present them. Many cake designers offer pedestals and serving plates for rent, but those can be quite expensive and you have to arrange for their return. My solution is a quick and easy tiered cake stand that assembles in minutes and can be thrown away right after the reception.

All of the supplies are readily available at craft and party supply stores and the cake boards can be decorated to suit any theme.

Get Your Craft On:
Made for Your Maid

Although this is super-simple to make on your own, you'll want to have a helper to assemble the cake tower and add the cupcakes at the reception. You'll have enough going on as you get ready for the ceremony!

Supplies Needed

- Cardboard cake boards, available at craft and party supply stores, in sizes 8 inches, 10 inches, and 14 inches (round or square, your preference)
- 2 acrylic or glass drinking glasses, 6 inches to 8 inches tall, clear or color
- Hot-glue gun and glue
- Decorative paper in the color of your choice (scrapbook paper or wrapping paper works well)
- Ribbon or fancy trim
- Spray adhesive

DIRECTIONS:

1. Cover the top of each cake board with your decorative paper. Don't stress about your paper selection. The paper will be covered, for the most part, with cupcakes. Most of your guests won't even see it. Spray adhesive on the top board and stick paper to the adhesive. Smooth it down with your fingers. Trim away any excess paper.

2. The drinking glasses serve as the supports between layers of cake board. If the glasses are larger at the opening than at the bottom, turn them upside down. Using the larger end as the bottom generally helps with structural support. Want to surprise your guests? Place small items in the glasses! You can insert something like live plants (ferns and succulents are perfect), vintage bride and groom figurines, silk flowers, or a photo of the bride and groom.

   Place a continuous string of hot glue along the top rim of the glass (drawing a). Immediately place the smallest cake board on top of the glass, making sure it's centered (drawing b). Now apply a string of hot glue to the bottom rim and place it, centered, on the

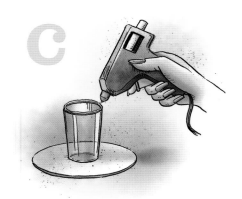

next cardboard cake board layer (drawing c). Glue the second glass to the bottom of this layer (drawing d). Finish the structure by gluing the bottom piece in place on the remaining cake board piece.

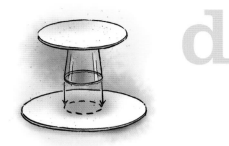

3. Ah, the last step! Decorate the edge of the top two cake boards by hot gluing ribbon or trim around the circumference of the boards (drawing e). That's it. You're now ready to load up your cupcake tower with cupcakes.

Tips & Hints:

-   Cardboard cake boards come in a variety of sizes, from 4 inches to more than 20 inches. The larger the boards you use, the more support they'll need. Either use larger (wider) glasses or more glasses to stabilize the layers.

-   Glasses aren't the only things you can use as support. Vases, candleholders, wooden blocks, glass bottles, or glass blocks (from your local home improvement center) all make great looking (and affordable) supports.

-   Stuck for centerpiece ideas? The cupcake stand can be used as a centerpiece. Display favors, plants, or candles for an easy table decoration.

Cost Comparison

Disposable cardboard cupcake stands can be found for around $40. This version costs less than $10.

Store Cost:	Your Cost:
$40	$10

CRYSTAL DROP *Cake Jewelry*

I'm totally hooked on celebrity weddings. Not that I'm invited to any, mind you. Rather, I scour the glossy magazines and celebrity gossip sites for the latest wedding news from the rich and famous. It's my guilty pleasure and a great way to spot future trends in the industry.

One of my favorite celebrity weddings was that of Carmen Electra and Dave Navarro. I thought they perfectly combined sophistication and elegance with roguish rocker charm. Even though the union of those two crazy kids didn't last, they sure left behind some cool touches.

An element from their wedding inspired the use of crystals as part of cake decorations. It's a simple and stunning detail for your perfect wedding—and it's easy, too! All you'll need for these crystal drops are some wire, some chandelier crystals, a pair of wire cutters, and pliers. Each takes just a minute to complete.

Shop around for the best prices on chandelier crystals. They vary widely in price and in shipping cost. Be very careful about using vintage chandelier crystals. Many were made of leaded crystal, which should under no circumstances be used on your cake.

Going Solo

The cake jewelry is pretty darned easy to make. Set aside an hour or so on the weekend to spend some quality time with your wire cutters and pliers.

Supplies Needed

- 18-gauge to 20-gauge stainless steel or jewelry wire
- 1-inch to 1½-inch crystal or plastic chandelier drops in the colors of your choice
- Wire cutters
- Round-nose pliers

DIRECTIONS:

1. Most chandelier drops come with a little hook in the top crystal. Use a pair of round-nose pliers to close the hook to make a loop (drawing a). Repeat this for all of your crystal drops. Aren't they gorgeous?

2. Cut a piece of wire for each the crystals. Cut various lengths, from 8 inches to 12 inches. Use your fingers to straighten each piece as best as you can. Some of the wires will be uncooperative and will fight to keep their kinks and curves. That's OK. It adds character.

3. On each piece of wire, create a basic jewelry loop (see The Basics: Tools & Techniques, page 14, for instructions). Before closing the loop, thread the open end of the wire through the loop you created with the crystal hanger (drawing b). Close the loop with round-nose pliers.

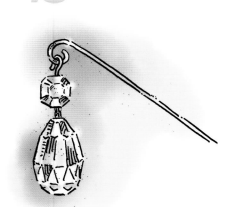

4. Now, holding the loop you just created in one hand and the wire stem in the other, create a subtle arc in the wire so the crystals drop down (drawing c). I know, I know. You just straightened all of your wire! The bend you're creating is very subtle and serves to make the crystals arc away from the cake. It's a really stunning effect.

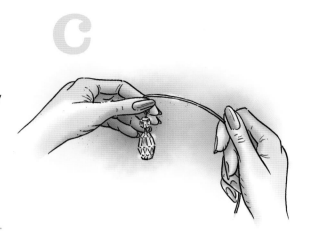

5. Insert the finished pieces into your cake. You're done!

Tips & Hints:

- Leave the final placement of the jewelry at the reception to your wedding coordinator or caterer, if you can.

- Chandelier drops come in a variety of shapes, sizes, and colors.

- Most wedding cake layers are between 2 inches and 5 inches tall. If you use fresh flowers between layers, the overall length of your cake jewelry should be between 6 inches and 12 inches to give them enough height to rise above the cake and flowers. If you're not using flowers between layers, wires 2 inches to 4 inches taller than the cake layer should be sufficient.

- Instead of drops made from crystal, which can be too heavy for delicate cakes, buy ones made of plastic or Lucite®. They can be found at chandelier shops and many craft stores. If you use heavier crystals, use 18-gauge wire for better support.

Cost Comparison

Similar cake jewelry retails for $4 to $8 each. The DIY Bride version costs under $1 to make.

Store Cost:	Your Cost:
$4–$8	$1

STANDING *Table Numbers*

Few things strike terror into the hearts of mild-mannered wedding guests as much as the seating arrangement. "Where's my table?" is first and foremost on their minds when they walk into the reception.

Put your friends and family at ease with these simple and easy-to-read table numbers. Although this isn't the most challenging project you can take on, it's one that your guests are sure to appreciate, and it won't break your budget. This takes just a few minutes to create and assemble and can be made for mere pennies.

The supplies can be found at any craft or office supply store and they can be customized to suit any décor or theme.

Get Your Craft On:
Party Time!

Although you probably can do this one on your own, a few helping hands will make the tasks of folding, cutting, and adhering fly right on by.

Supplies Needed

- 3 sheets 8½-inch by 11-inch card-stock in the colors of your choice
- 6 sheets decorative paper in the colors of your choice, 4½ inches by 6½ inches
- 6 sheets white cardstock, 4 inches by 6 inches
- Double-sided tape
- Computer with Microsoft Word
- Printer

STATION 1: Cutting the Cardstock
This person gets to cut the cardstock to size.

STATION 2: Printing
This is a low-maintenance position made just for you.

STATION 3: Folding
While your table numbers are printing, chip in to help fold the cardstock bases.

STATION 4: Assembly
Set up an assembly line. Each person adds a layer to the base card.

Cost Comparison

Custom-printed table numbers can easily cost upward of $3 each. These cost about $0.50 using a good-quality paper.

Store Cost:	*Your Cost:*
$3	**50¢**

DIRECTIONS

1. First create the printed table number or table name. Open Microsoft Word and create a new document. Under the Paper tab in the Page Setup dialog box, select Custom Size from the Paper Size options. Set the custom page size for 4 inches wide by 6 inches high. Click OK.

2. In the blank document, type in the table name or number. Adjust the font size to the maximum that fits in the space. Each font will be different, so experiment to find out what size, font, and color works best for you. Do use a font that's clear and easy for all of your guests to read.

3. Select all (Control key + A) and hit the Center button in the horizontal alignment toolbar. This will center the text on the card.

4. Print six copies of this document onto cardstock.

5. Create the stand by folding each piece of 8½-inch by 11-inch cardstock in half (drawing a).

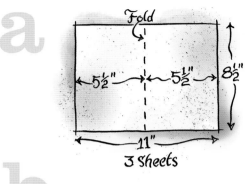

6. To give your table number some pop and pizzazz, you'll add a layer of decorative paper behind it. This is called a mat. Put a line of adhesive on the back of one of the pieces of 4½-inch by 6½-inch decorative paper, along the top and bottom edges. Place this piece in the center of one side of the folded stand you just made. Repeat for the other side (drawing b). Now apply a long strip of double-sided tape to the back of the white cardstock with the number. Place this onto the center of the 4½-inch by 6½-inch decorative paper (drawing c). Do this for all six panels of the stand.

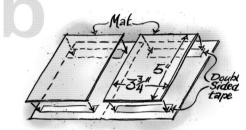

7. On the back side of each of the cardstock pieces, apply a line of double-stick tape near the top and bottom edges.

8. Stick the back sides of the cardstock to each other, from left to right (drawing d).

9. Now, apply a long strip of double-sided tape to the back of the white cardstock. Place this onto the center of the 4½-inch by 6½-inch decorative paper. Apply double-sided tape to the back of the decorative paper and firmly press it onto one of the panels of the cardstock stand. Do this for all six panels of the stand.

Tips & Hints:

• Have guests sign their names to the table numbers. After the reception, place them into a scrapbook or memory box.

FLOATING *Table Number Centerpiece*

I'm a minimalist kind of girl when it comes to table settings. Standard reception table décor is usually overly fussy and way too crowded for my liking. By the time the centerpiece, glass-ware, favors, place cards, table numbers, dinnerware, napkins, purses, and elbows of my fellow guests are all plopped on the table, there's little room to move around comfortably during the meal. Give me simplicity (and space), please!

For this project, let's combine the table number and centerpiece into a piece of functional table décor. By submerging the table number into a vase of water, it takes on an artsy look that can be embellished and translated into any theme. Change out sand and shells on the bottom for something like colored stones or submerged flowers for a completely different feel. Any type and color of papers can be used, because they're protected by the laminate sheets. This is a great project to play around with color and design.

Get Your Craft On:
It's a Girl Thing

This is a quick and easy project for a small group. Invite a few friends over for an evening of crafts and cosmos. Slip the first season of *Sex and the City* into your DVD player and bond with your closest gal pals.

Supplies Needed

- 1 clear cylindrical, round, or square vase, approximately 10 inches to 14 inches tall and 6 inches to 8 inches in diameter
- White cardstock, 8½ inches by 11 inches
- Decorative papers in the colors of your choice, 8½ inches by 11 inches
- Clear self-adhesive laminating sheets, available at office supply stores
- Needle or small hole punch
- Double-sided adhesive
- Stones or pebbles, enough to fill 1 inch on the bottom of the vase
- Craft wire, 24 gauge
- Water
- Computer with Microsoft Word
- Printer

STATION 1: Cutting Cardstock
Cut the cardstock to size. The more uniform the cuts, the better the laminate sheets will bond in later steps

STATION 2: Printing
This is a great job for you. You can load the printer and step away to socialize while the numbers print.

STATION 3: Decorating the Table Numbers
Get everyone involved in this step because it's so much fun!

STATION 4: Laminating
Who's the person with steady hands and the patience of a saint? This is her job.

STATION 5: Punching Holes and Filling the Vases with Rocks
This is a great job for anyone who wants something easy to do.

DIRECTIONS

1. Get the party started! Cut the white cardstock in quarters to get 4¼-inch by 5½-inch pieces.

2. Open Microsoft Word and create a new document. From the File menu, select Page Setup and then Custom Size under Page Size in the Paper tab. Set the custom page size for 4¼ inches wide by 5½ inches tall. Click OK.

3. Set the margin spacing to 0.25 inch for the left and right margins and the top and bottom margins. Insert your table number or table name into the document. Save the document and then print two copies onto the white cardstock. Play around with different fonts and sizes. My only suggestion is to use a large font that's not too ornate for your table numbers. It's nice to do what you can to help your guests find their tables.

4. Adhere the two table numbers together, back to back (drawing a).

5. Cut two pieces of laminate sheet ½ inch larger on all sides than your table numbers. In this case, it's 4¾ inches by 6 inches. Place one side of the table number in the center of one of the laminate sheets (drawing b). Turn the table number over and affix the second laminate sheet directly on top (drawing c). Working with laminate sheets can sometimes be tricky. They stick to everything and everything sticks to them. Go slow when peeling off the back and use a steady, firm pressure when placing the number onto the laminate sheet.

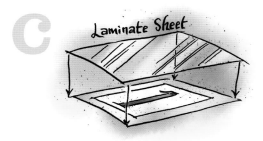

Laminate Sheet

6. With a bone folder or your fingertips, press the edges of the laminate sheets together, smoothing out any air bubbles or creases.

Laminate Sheet

7. Punch a small hole through the bottom of the table number, about ½ inch from the bottom edge.

8. Hang in there! You're almost done. Cut a 4-inch length of craft wire from the spool. Loop one end through the hole in the table number and twist to secure it. Wrap the free end around a heavy stone and place it in the vase (drawing d). If you don't plan to use stones in your vase, use a dab of hot glue to secure the end of the wire to the container's bottom.

9. Place an inch or two of pebbles, marbles, or stones in the bottom of the base. Fill with water. The table number will rise and be suspended upright in the water (drawing e).

Tips & Hints:

- Leave the final placement of the table numbers at the reception to your wedding coordinator, caterer, or handy helpers, if you can.

- The combination of the glass vase and water will make the table number appear larger than it actually is.

- Use photos, postcards, or other ephemera inside the laminate sheets. You can decorate the table number with stamps, glitter, or other flat objects as well.

- The vases look great with stones, floating candles, sand, floating flowers, or fake grass secured to the bottom.

- The vases can also double as pedestals. Place plates on top to set mini-cakes or cupcakes on. Or you can set floral arrangements on top.

Cost Comparison

I haven't seen anything like this on the market. Florists charge anywhere from $30 to $75 for a simple centerpiece. The DIY Bride version costs about $17.

Store Cost:	Your Cost:
$30–$75	$17

table seven

Photos of you and your sweetie can make a fun focal point for the table. Use a different shot for each centerpiece.

CORK *Place Card Holders*

Are you and your beloved the resident wine snobs in your circle of friends? While your pals are fine with *Chateau Whatever*, do you obsess over the perfect wine pairings with the fervor of the finest sommelier? When it came time to dream up a theme for your reception, was the obvious choice a vineyard-inspired fete to invoke the feeling of those deliciously intimate dinners you had on your last vacation to California's wine country?

If so, the perfect little place card holder to accentuate your vineyard theme is, of course, made of a wine cork. Genius! And oh-so-simple.

For this project, we used new corks, but you can substitute corks from your favorite bottles of vino. Just make sure you've washed and dried them thoroughly before you turn them into place card holders. Corks can be found in bulk at home-brew shops and online. Try eBay for super-cheap used corks in bulk.

Get Your Craft On:
It's a Girl Thing

Bring your handy helpers together for a wine and craft night. You provide your favorite vintage, some yummy cheese, and all the craft supplies. They provide the labor. It's a win-win situation.

Supplies Needed

- Wine corks
- Craft knife with a straight blade
- Towel
- Green cardstock (or other colors of your choice)
- Purple cardstock (or other colors of your choice)
- White cardstock, 8½ inches by 11 inches
- Rubber stamp
- Green ink (or other colors of your choice)
- Purple glitter glue (or other colors of your choice)
- Paper cutter
- Double-sided tape
- Cutting mat or cutting board

STATION 1: Cut the Bottoms of the Corks
Who do you trust with sharp knives? Put them on the first task. Remember to protect your table with a cutting mat or clean cutting board from the kitchen.

STATION 2: Cut the Slits in the Corks
It may seem like an easy job, but this one takes a little skill. Find out who has steady hands in your group and turn them loose at this station.

STATION 3: Cut the Cardstock
This is a great job for one or two friends to share.

STATION 4: Rubber Stamping
Save this step for your artsy buddies. Although stamping isn't hard, this step is perfect for anyone with a keen eye for detail.

STATION 5: Assemble the Cardstock Layers
This is the easiest step. Almost anyone can handle sticking the cardstock layers together.

DIRECTIONS

1. Cork is tricky to cut and it tends to slip under the blade. Use the sharpest blade you can find and put an old towel under the cork to help prevent slipping. Cut a strip of cork away to create a flat surface that will be the bottom of the place card holder. Use a craft knife to cut off ¼ inch along the length of the cork (drawing a).

2. Set the cork on its newly created bottom. Along the top edge, cut a groove into the cork from side to side (drawing a). The groove should go about ½ inch into the cork to give adequate support for the place card. Use a craft knife for a smoother cut.

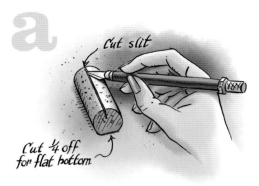

3. To create the place cards, cut the cardstock as follows: Green cardstock—4 inches by 3¾ inches; Purple cardstock—3½ inches by 3¼ inches; Cream cardstock—3 inches by 2¾ inches.

4. Next, decorate and write (or print) a guest's name onto the cream cardstock. To decorate with a rubber stamp, apply ink to the stamp and then press the stamp onto the cardstock using firm, even pressure. Set the cardstock aside to dry. Then apply drops of glitter glue to accent any shapes or design elements. Set the card aside so the glue can completely dry. (This can take a few hours.)

5. Attach the cardstock together, in layers, with double-sided tape. Apply the purple cardstock on top of the green cardstock and then the cream on top of the purple, centering each layer. Set the place card into the top slit in the cork.

Tips & Hints:

- The straighter the cork, the easier it'll be to cut. Beware, some sparkling wines and champagnes have odd-shaped corks.

- Wash used corks in warm soapy water and let them dry completely before you craft with them. This kills lingering bacteria and washes away sediment that stains your linens.

- Leave the final placement of the place holders at the reception to your wedding coordinator, caterer, or handy helpers, if you can.

Cost Comparison

Specialty retailers charge $1.20 or more per cork place card holder. Mine, including the place card, cost about $0.25 using brand new corks. Used corks can be even cheaper when purchased in bulk.

Store Cost:	Your Cost:
$1.20	25¢

SEATING *Chart*

The United Nations could take a few pointers from you. You just brought together over 100 of your most eccentric friends and family members into the perfectly harmonious territory that will be your wedding reception. Sure, it took several grueling hours of negotiation and careful plotting with your beloved, but you just attained the highest level of creativity and diplomacy imaginable: seating assignments.

After the countless hours you undoubtedly spent arranging the perfect tablemates for each of your guests, you'll thank me for this blissfully simple project. The supplies are easily found at any craft store or art supply house and the chart assembles in just a few minutes.

The beauty of this type of seating chart is that individual table cards can be revised at a moment's notice should any last-minute changes arise in your guest list. The supplies are inexpensive, too. You can easily make this for under $15.

Supplies Needed

- 1 sheet foam board, 32 inches by
  40 inches, available at craft and art
  supply stores
- Light green cardstock (or other
  colors of your choice), 8½ inches by
  11 inches
- White cardstock, 8½ inches by
  11 inches
- Light green ribbon (or other colors
  of your choice), ¼-inch wide
- Double-sided tape
- Paper cutter
- Computer with Microsoft Word
- Printer
- Scissors

DIRECTIONS

1. First create the list of guests for each table. Open Microsoft Word
   and create a new document. Under the Paper tab in the Page
   Setup dialog box, select Custom Size from the Paper Size list.
   Set the custom page size for 4 inches wide by 6 inches. Click OK.
   Note: Your page size may vary depending on how many cards you
   use for your seating chart.

2. Type in the table number and the guest list for each table on a
   page in your document.

3. Print the document onto precut 4-inch by 6-inch white cardstock.

4. For the top plaque with the couple's name and wedding date, I
   used a sheet of 8½-inch by 11-inch cardstock cut to 8½ inches
   by 4 inches. For the head table, I printed the names of the bridal
   party onto a 4-inch by 6-inch sheet of cardstock, but used a landscape orientation when printing.

5. The next step is to create a mat for each of the printed pieces
   from the light green cardstock backing. To do this, I cut the green
   cardstock to ½ inch larger
   than the dimensions of each
   card. For example, to mat
   the 4-inch by 6-inch cards, I
   cut the green cardstock to
   4½ inches by 6½ inches.

6. Before you attach the white
   cardstock to its mat, tie a
   ribbon around the top of the
   white cardstock (drawing a). I
   used about 12 inches of ribbon
   for each 4-inch by 6-inch card.

7. Now you'll mat the white cards to their light green backing pieces. Apply a line of double-sided tape to the back of the white cards. Place them onto the center of the light green cards. Press them down firmly to adhere them in place (drawing b).

8. The last step is to attach the finished cards to the foam board. Apply a couple of lines of double-sided tape to the back of each card. Press the cards firmly into place onto the foam board.

Tips & Hints

- Leave the final placement of your seating chart at the reception to your wedding coordinator, caterer, or handy helper, if you can.

- Foam board can easily be covered with fabric, acrylic craft paints, or decorative papers.

- Use decorative pushpins to hold the table cards in place instead of double-sided tape. Stationery and craft stores sell pins in all sorts of shapes, designs, and sizes. Try rhinestone pins for an elegant look or plastic daisies for an informal garden theme.

- Foam board is available in colors other than white. Most craft stores will carry foam board in primary colors and black.

Cost Comparison	
Custom-designed seating charts cost over $100. This one costs less than $15 to make.	
Store Cost:	Your Cost:
$100	**$15**

LUMINARIA *Tree*

Winter weddings get shortchanged in the décor department. Couples getting married in chilly months often get the wide and varied options of Christmas decorations or something snowflakey.

For that cosmopolitan couple who wants something wintry on the cheap, a gathering of branches placed in a beautiful vase is a simple way to give a table some sophisticated warmth.

The beauty of this centerpiece is that it's made of branches scavenged from the yard, spray painted white, and arranged in an elegant, colorful vase. Two glittery birds are nestled in the branches for a little extra color, along with cute paper luminaries that illuminate the table.

I love this project because it's modern and fresh. You'll love the project because it's chic style for a small budget.

Bring together a small group for the painting and assembly of the centerpieces. Because the paint will need to dry for a few hours, break the task up into a couple of teams on two separate days. Have Team One gather, prune, and paint the branches. Team Two will be in charge of cutting and assembling the luminaria.

Supplies Needed:

- 1 vase, 10 inches to 14 inches tall
- Tree branches, 16 inches to 20 inches tall; branches from cherry, apple, and aspen trees are good choices
- Silver jewelry wire, 24 gauge
- Wire cutters
- Silver paper, 8½ inches by 11 inches
- Paper cutter
- ⅛-inch hole punch
- ¾-inch circle punch
- Sand or pea gravel
- White spray paint
- Garden shears

DIRECTIONS:

1. Gather branches together and cut them to fit inside of your vase. A good rule of thumb for branch height is that they should extend about 8 inches to 12 inches above the top rim of the vase. Don't be afraid to play around with branch height and fullness to create an arrangement that works well with your branches and vase combination. For a skinny vase, you'll want something stark and minimal. A wider vase will need a fuller set of branches to give it proper balance.

2. Spray paint the branches white. It's important to do this outside and on a protected surface, such as sheets of newspaper or cardboard. To help prevent scratching off each layer of paint, work in sections. Set the branch down and spray the front. Let it dry completely. Once the paint has dried, gently turn the branch over and work on the other side. It may take a few coats of paint to get even coverage. Remember to spray in a well-ventilated area on a day that's not windy.

3. While the branches are drying, create the paper luminarias. Cut the silver paper into strips 8½ inches wide by 4 inches tall (drawing a). You'll get two luminarias from each sheet of paper.

4. Fold the paper in half along the 8½-inch length. Crease the paper, then unfold it (drawing b).

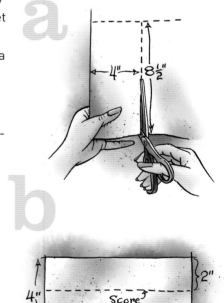

5. Turn the paper ½ inch, and fold it at 2 inches, 4 inches, 6 inches, and 8 inches from the short edge. Crease the folds and then lay the paper flat again (drawing c).

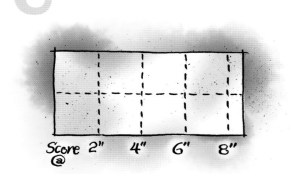

6. Use scissors to cut off the smallest rectangle (2 inches by ½ inch) created by the score lines.

7. Cut each 2-inch score mark along the bottom on the 8½-inch side of the paper (drawing d). You will be making three cuts, one along each of the 2-inch score marks. Do not cut beyond the long score mark running the length of the 8½-inch side.

8. Fold along all score marks.

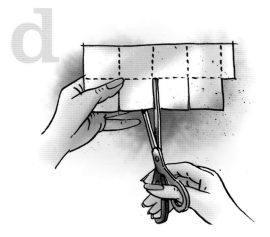

9. Place a section of double-sided tape along the 2-inch by ½-inch flap.

10. Fold up the four 2-inch by 2-inch pieces to create the bottom of the box. Use double-sided tape on the last 2-inch by 2-inch piece to seal the bottom of the box.

11. With a ⅛-inch hole punch, punch holes in two sides (opposite one another) of the luminaria, about ½ inch down from the top. On the two remaining sides, punch ¾-inch holes with the other punch to create "windows" for the light to shine through (drawing e).

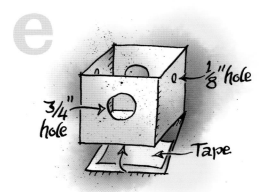

12. Cut lengths of wire 4 inches long. Thread wire through each of the 1/8-inch holes and twist the ends to secure it (drawing f).

13. Pour sand into the vase, about half full. Insert branches into the sand so that they stand upright. Add more sand if you need more stability.

14. Insert the tea lights into the luminaria and hang them on the branches. Light the candles with a gas torch lighter. They can be found at hardware stores and even grocery stores near the barbeque supplies.

Tips & Hints:

- For the final placement of the trees at the reception, you'll need a set (or two) of helpers on the wedding day to bring all the pieces together as centerpieces. You can count on each centerpiece taking a full 5 minutes to assemble. Get started at least an hour before the ceremony is to begin to get everything finished on time.

- Branches are free—if you know where to look. Ask friends, family, and neighbors to save their tree prunings for you. Some local parks will allow you to collect fallen branches (but usually require a permit to cut from live trees).

- If you want uniformity in your branches, order them from a florist or a floral supply house. They'll source a single type of branch in suitable sizes for you.

- The branches needn't be painted white—or at all. Leave them unpainted for a natural, rustic look or paint them any other color for something unexpected.

- Any type of tall vase or container will work for this project. Paint terra cotta pots for a cheap alternative to glass vases. Galvanized buckets work well, too. Plastic planters from garden supply centers come in a variety of styles from sleek to ornate to fit your theme.

- Add glitter to the branches or fake blossoms for extra sparkle and pizzazz.

- Check with your venue before you buy your candles. Many halls do not allow open flame. If yours is one of them, there are now battery-operated tea lights on the market that work perfectly in the luminaria. They can be found at major craft stores.

Cost Comparison

Florists charge over $60 for custom branch centerpieces. Ours costs about $30.

Store Cost:	Your Cost:
$60	$30

SPLIT BAMBOO *Centerpiece*

If I had to describe my personal decorating style, I'd sum it up as Shabby-Tropical-Asian-Chic, or maybe even Bali-Kitsch. I have a profound weakness for anything rustic, aged, and Asian, much to the chagrin of my husband, who has his own inclinations toward things of leopard print. We don't always see eye to eye on our home décor, but we both fell in love with this centerpiece.

With a definite Asian influence, this bamboo centerpiece is elegant without being stuffy. The minimalist design is modern but the weathered bamboo gives it warmth and personality. What's really great is that it can transform from an Asian theme to an outdoor theme by changing the filler inside each of the pockets.

You will have to put in a little muscle for this project. Cutting the bamboo in half and into sections is the hardest part. A sharp sawblade and some helping hands to steady the bamboo while you cut will make this project easier.

Bamboo poles can be found in abundance at many home and garden centers during the summer months. Out of season, they can be ordered online, but be careful. Shipping rates can be double the price of the poles themselves.

Get Your Craft On:
Where the Boys Are

Save your sanity and pass this off to the manly men of the wedding party. Best for outdoors, this project is perfect for a groomsmen barbeque. Spark up the grill, chill the microbrews, and whip out the tools. Divvy up the tasks as follows to make light work of the bamboo:

Supplies Needed

- Bamboo pole, 4 inches to 5 inches in diameter, available at home and garden centers, import stores, and floral supply shops
- Fine-blade saw
- Sandpaper
- Wood file, 8-inch to 10-inch flat, available at hardware stores
- Paste wax, found at hardware stores
- Rock salt, found at home improvement and hardware stores in bulk
- Tea lights

STATION 1: Cutting the Bamboo to Size
Have a couple of guys cut the bamboo into segments.

STATION 2: Splitting the Bamboo
It takes a couple of coordinated people to handle the splitting chore. One person can hold the bamboo piece while the other saws it in half.

STATION 3: Filing the Bamboo
This lucky chap is in charge of putting that baby-bottom smooth finish to the cut edges of the bamboo.

STATION 4: Applying Wax to the Bamboo (or Painting)
You know that friend who spends hours every Saturday morning hand washing and waxing his car? This is the project for him.

For a beachy theme, fill the bamboo with sand and polished stones.

DIRECTIONS

1. Sawing bamboo can be a little taxing. Go slow and use the sharpest blade you can. Using the fine-blade saw, cut the bamboo pole into 36-inch segments, leaving the bamboo nodes intact. The nodes are the horizontal lines across the bamboo pole that create compartments within the bamboo stalk.

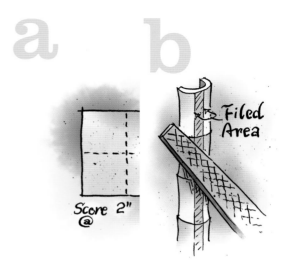

Score 2" @

Filed Area

2. Saw each segment in half lengthwise (drawing a). Bamboo is hollow, except for the nodes. Getting through the cavities is usually very easy. The nodes take a little muscle. Sand away any splinters or uneven patches along the sawed edges.

3. To prevent the bamboo from rolling, use a file to create a flat surface on the bottom exterior of the bamboo (drawing b). Bamboo can be filed with a regular 8-inch to 10-inch flat wood file. Hold the file parallel to the bamboo's grain and press the file firmly onto the wood as you move it back and forth. Warning: Filing against the bamboo's grain may cause it to splinter. Splintering isn't a big deal; just sand down the splintered area with a fine-grit sandpaper.

4. Apply a coat of paste wax to the exterior of the bamboo. This will give the bamboo a rich, professional-quality finish. It helps preserve the wood, too.

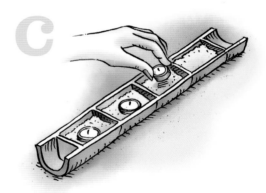

5. Fill each compartment of the bamboo with rock salt. Place tea lights onto the salt and light the wicks (drawing c). I suggest using a tea light with at least a 4-hour burning time. They're a little more expensive but you're guaranteed to have lit candles throughout the entire reception.

Tips & Hints

- Leave the final assembly of the bamboo centerpiece to your wedding coordinator or caterer, if you can. If not, have a couple of dedicated helpers on hand to put everything together at the reception.
- Summer months offer the best selection of bamboo at your local garden centers.

Cost Comparison

A custom bamboo centerpiece will cost around $80 from a florist. Our version cost about $25.

Store Cost:	Your Cost:
$80	**$25**

RIBBON-BOUND *Guest Book*

The guest book is a misunderstood wedding accessory. Usually overly fussy in design, it's a book many think of only as way to remember who attended the wedding—and they use it as such. A pity, really, because it's a precious heirloom-in-waiting.

Instead of opting for an over-the-top (and pricey) book, create your own handmade beauty. With just a few supplies found at most craft and art stores, you can make a custom creation that will last a lifetime. There are no rules for this project, so have fun combining papers and ribbon. You can even use lightweight fabrics as a covering instead of decorative papers—a perfect use for your mom's wedding gown or hand-me-down hankies.

At the wedding, invite your guests to capture their thoughts and wishes by leaving creative accounts of the wedding day. You'll find out what your guests really think of you and you'll have some fun and delightful entries to read later. (Who knew you had so many talented writer pals?)

Get Your Craft On:

Going Solo

This is a great project for a quiet afternoon or evening. Grab your drink of choice, put on your "guilty pleasure" music, and enjoy some crafty "me" time.

Supplies Needed

- Chip board, single thickness, available at art supply stores
- Craft knife
- Heavy-duty hole punch
- Watercolor paper, 22 inches by 30 inches
- Spray adhesive
- Scissors
- Ruler
- Pencil
- Double-sided adhesive strips
- Ribbon
- Japanese washi paper or other decorative papers, 8½ inches by 11 inches or larger
- Printer paper, for the inside pages

DIRECTIONS

1. Using a straightedge (or ruler) and craft knife, cut the chipboard into two 8½-inch by 5½-inch pieces.

2. Cut 1 inch off of each 8½-inch side. Save the 1-inch pieces. You'll now have two pieces measuring 7½ inches by 5½ inches and two pieces measuring 1 inch by 5½ inches (drawing a).

3. From the watercolor paper, cut two pieces measuring 18 inches long by 6½ inches tall. Lay one of the pieces flat on your work surface. Make a crease in the paper 1 inch from the left-hand side. Make another crease along the top of the paper, ½ inch from the top. Now, make another crease, ½ inch from the bottom. Do not crease the right-hand side yet. Repeat this step for the other piece of watercolor paper (drawing b).

4. Glue the chipboard pieces into place. Brush a light coating of glue onto one side of the 1-inch by 5½-inch chipboard piece. Place it glue side down onto the watercolor paper, to the right of the vertical crease you made on the left-hand side of the paper and under the top crease line. Apply glue to the 7½-inch by 5½-inch piece of chipboard and place it next to the 1-inch by 5 ½-inch strip you just laid down, but leave a small gap, about ⅛ inch, between the two pieces. This creates a hinge that will allow the book to open easily. Let the glue dry. While you're waiting, you can repeat this step for the remaining chipboard and watercolor paper (drawing c).

5. After the glue dries, fold the watercolor paper over the chipboard to cover it. To create sharp corners, cut a diagonal (drawing d) line next to—but not right up against—the chipboard on the top and bottom edges of the left-hand side. This is called a miter cut. Apply adhesive to the 1-inch by 5½-inch chipboard and fold the flap of paper on the left over the chipboard. Smooth it down with your fingers to remove any air bubbles or bumps (drawing e).

The right-hand side of the chipboard is a little different. You won't miter the corners as you just did with the left side. Instead, cut a vertical line along the crease from the top of the paper to the top-edge of the chipboard. Do the same for the bottom of the paper as well. Once your paper is cut, apply adhesive to the entire exposed area of chipboard. Fold down the top and bottom flaps. Smooth them out with your fingers. Now apply adhesive over the top and bottom flaps and fold the right-hand flap over the chipboard. Smooth it down to remove any wrinkles or air bubbles. The paper should be taut and wrinkle-free. Repeat these steps for the other side of the book while the adhesive is drying. Use a small pair of scissors to trim away any excess bits of paper that may overhang the chipboard (drawing f).

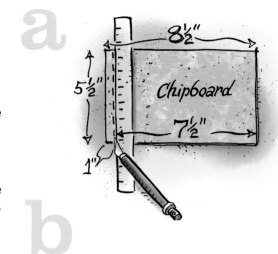

6. After the front and back covers are dry, punch four holes in the spine on each cover (drawing g). My advice is to punch one set of holes and use that as a template on the other cover so that the holes line up perfectly.

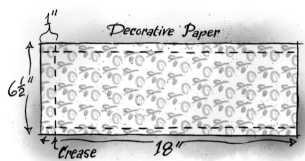

7. Now add a decorative paper sleeve to each cover. From a sheet of Japanese washi paper, cut two pieces, 7½ inches by 10¼ inches. On the inside of each cover, apply a line of adhesive along the top, about ¼ inch down. Do not cover the 1-inch spine piece, just the 7½-inch-wide area (drawing h). Attach the paper and flip the cover over. Apply a thin coat of adhesive on the front side of the cover and press the washi paper down, smoothing out any wrinkles or bubbles. Flip it over again and apply a full, even coat of adhesive on the inside of the cover. Press the paper into place. Cut away any overhanging pieces of paper. Repeat for the other cover. Set them aside to dry.

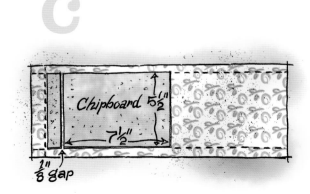

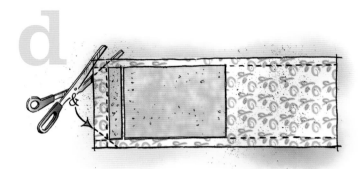

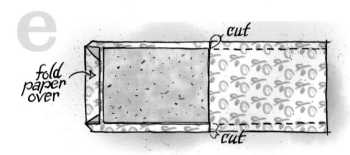

8. Cut sheets of printer paper to 8 inches by 5 inches. How many sheets you need depends on how many guests you're expecting. A good rule of thumb is one sheet for every five guests. Use one of your covers as the template for punching holes in the sheets of paper. Clamp the sheets together with a large binder clip to hold them in place for binding.

9. To finish up the guest book, bind the covers and inserts together. With a binding clip, hold the covers and inserts together, aligning the holes. Thread the ends of ribbon, from the bottom to the top, through each of the two center holes (drawing i). Now thread each end through the hole next to it, from the top to the bottom (drawing j). Now thread the ribbon back through the center holes (drawing k). Don't worry; it may seem funny but it secures the book together nicely and looks pretty. Tie the loose ends into a simple bow (double-knotted) and cut away any excess ribbon (drawing l).

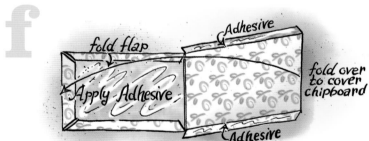

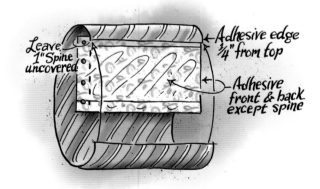

Tips & Hints:

- Leave the final placement of the guest book to your wedding coordinator, caterer, or handy helper, if you can.

- Fabrics work well in place of the washi paper. Lightweight silks, satins, and cottons are perfect and come in countless designs and colors.

- Heavy-duty hole punches can be found at scrapbook stores and art supply houses. They're more robust than regular office punches and make punching holes in chipboard a snap.

Cost Comparison

Hand-bound guest books cost upward of $40 at specialty retailers. Our version costs about $15, using imported Japanese papers.

Store Cost:	Your Cost:
$40	**$15**

i

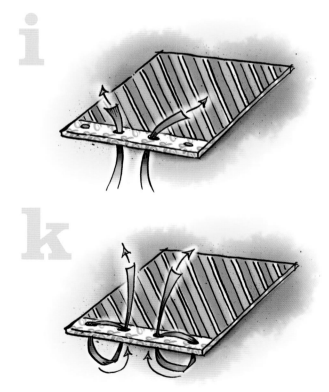

j

l

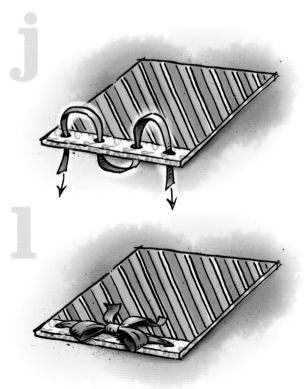

k

5 Giving with Style
Favors, Gifts & Goodies

Giving a little thank-you gift to your wedding guests, not to mention your bridesmaids and groomsmen, never goes out of fashion. Give back with style (and without breaking the bank), whether it's yummy fudge or chic candles as favors, or stylish totes and cool cufflinks as thank-you gifts for your wedding party.

FUDGE *Favors*

Forget monogrammed tchotchkes. Don't even think of almonds swathed in puffs of tulle. Go luxe, dear readers, with favors that will delight the most finicky of guests. Try delicious stacked "cakes" of homemade fudge.

Wedding guests love edible favors, and you can never, ever go wrong with chocolate. Your guests will feel spoiled and a little naughty for indulging in something so rich and decadent.

For this project start a few days ahead of the reception and allow for plenty of space in the refrigerator to keep your treats cool until serving time. The process is a bit time consuming, but the sugar rush is totally worth it in the end.

The keys to good fudge are using the highest-quality chocolate you can afford, letting the batches cool to room temperature before you place them in the fridge, and slicing with a very sharp chef's knife for easy cutting.

Get Your Craft On:
Family Bonding

In this case, too many cooks *don't* spoil the pot. Enlist the help of all of your favorite home cooks for creating this project. They're all welcome to lend their hands and kitchens to your cause. Assign helpers to make a batch or two of fudge. Others can come together to cut the squares and to assemble the towers.

Supplies Needed
(for 1 dozen favors)

- 2 pounds semi-sweet chocolate chips
- 4 tablespoons butter
- 2—14-ounce cans of sweetened condensed milk
- Medium pot
- Large metal mixing bowl
- Waxed paper
- 1 nonstick jelly roll pan, 18 inches by 13 inches by 1 inch
- Sharp chef's knife
- Ruler
- Toothpicks
- Crystals in your choice of colors, 6mm

DIRECTIONS

1. Line the jelly roll pan with waxed paper.

2. Fill a medium-size pot with 1 inch of water. Bring the water to a full boil, then reduce the heat to low. The water should be very hot and steaming but no longer boiling.

3. Place the metal mixing bowl on top of the pot. The bottom of the bowl should be suspended above the water level, not sitting directly in the water. If the bottom of the bowl gets too hot, the chocolate will burn and completely ruin the fudge.

4. In the bowl place the chocolate chips, butter, and condensed milk. Melt the ingredients together and mix until they're smooth. Constantly stir the mixture to prevent it from overheating and burning.

5. Once the mixture is completely melted, pour the fudge into the jelly roll pan. Your fudge mixture should be smooth and gooey. With a spatula, spread the mixture evenly across the pan.

6. Set the fudge on the counter and cool to room temperature. After it's cool and begins to firm, cover the pan with plastic wrap and place the fudge into the refrigerator. Let the fudge completely chill and firm up. This will take at least two hours.

7. After the fudge cools, remove it from the pan by turning the pan gently upside down onto a cutting board or work surface.

8. Turn the fudge back upright and cut it into squares in sizes 1 inch by 1 inch, 1½ inches by 1½ inches, and 2 inches by 2 inches. Use the ruler to measure off the squares, and with the edge of a pairing or other sharp knife score the measurements into the fudge. Once your squares are all mapped out, cut them out with a large-blade chef's knife.

9. Stack the squares on top of each other to create a graduated cake shape (photo a).

10. Place a crystal on top of a toothpick (see drawing b). Insert the toothpick into the center of the fudge stack (see drawing c). Cut off any excess toothpick that protrudes from the bottom.

11. Keep the fudge towers chilled until ready to serve.

Tips & Hints

- Leave the final placement of your fudge favors to your wedding coordinator, caterer, or handy helpers, if you can.

- Splurge on the best chocolate you can buy.

- Keep the fudge in a cool place until you're ready to cut it. The firmer the fudge, the easier it will be to slice.

- Try using cookie cutters on the fudge. They're available in squares, circles, and dozens of other fun shapes.

- Sprinkle edible glitters over the cakes for a little sparkle.

- The fudge towers are sure to be a big hit with your guests. For easy and elegant presentation, try displaying them in clear take-out boxes or place them on paper doilies.

Place Crystal on Toothpick

Insert pick thru center

Cost Comparison

Godiva charges $38 per set of four for wedding cake–shaped chocolate favors. These fudge favors cost less than $0.75 each.

Store Cost:	Your Cost:
$38	75¢

VOTIVE *Candles and Matches*

Are you agonizing over what favors to give your guests? Edible or not? Useful or decorative? Monogrammed or not? Scented or unscented? Finding that little token of appreciation to bestow upon your guests can be near torture. I agonized for weeks over what favors to give at my reception, and years later I think I finally have the whole favors thing figured out: Whatever you give will be fine.

That said, I have a few quick rules about favors. Make them useful or edible, keep them as lightly scented as possible, make them attractive enough for the guests to want to take home, and resist the urge to permanently monogram them with your initials. (If you *must* monogram, darlings, add it to the packaging.)

Candles are universally appreciated and generally well-received as favors. Paired with a coordinating box of matches, they're a decorative and useful favor that most guests can appreciate.

These votive candles can be incorporated into nearly any décor or theme and are inexpensive to make.

Gather your moms and maids together for an afternoon of crafts and bonding. Make enough templates ahead of time so that each helper has her own. This'll help speed up the cutting process and allow your helpers more time for decorating and chatting.

Supplies Needed
- Glass votive cups with a smooth surface
- Matchboxes
- Decorative papers in the colors of your choice
- ⅛-inch peel-off liner adhesive tape
- Scissors or a paper cutter
- Pencil
- Cardboard or sheet of heavy cardstock

STATION 1: Candles
Have half of your helpers at the candle station. They're in charge of cutting the paper and decorating the candles. Have one or two finished candles on hand to serve as samples or inspiration pieces.

STATION 2: Matchboxes
The other half of your crew is in charge of decorating the matchboxes. Like with the candles, have a few premade ones to serve as samples.

DIRECTIONS

1. To get started on this project, you need to create a template for the votive wrappers. Trust me, you want a template. Don't skip this part! It makes cutting the paper to the right dimension so easy. We love easy! Votive cups are available in a variety of sizes, shapes, and surface textures. Choose cups that have a smooth surface and that don't taper much from top to bottom. The straighter the cup, the easier it is to wrap it.

   If your votive cup is straight (the top circumference is equal to the bottom circumference), you may not need a template. Instead, it may be easier to cut strips directly from your paper with no tracing. To determine what size strips to cut, measure around the circumference of the cup and add ¼ inch to the length. Measure the height of the cup and cut the corresponding measurements from the decorative papers (drawing a).

Covering votive cups that taper from top to bottom is a bit trickier. There will be a slight curve to the top and bottom of the paper when it's cut.

To get the proper shape for your template, wrap a piece of scrap paper firmly around one of the votive cups and hold it in place. With a pencil, trace along the inner-top rim and bottom edge of the holder onto the paper. Unroll the paper and cut out the shape, extending the length ¼ inch to create a small overlap when the votive is wrapped. Copy the shape onto cardboard or heavy cardstock and cut it out to make a reusable template.

2. Once you determine the size and shape of the wraps, cut the wraps out of the decorative papers. Straight-edge scissors are the most obvious choice here, but decorative scissors found at craft stores are really fun. Try a small scalloped scissor or a pinking-edge for something unique.

3. To attach the papers to the votive cups, apply a length of ⅛-inch peel-off adhesive tape from top to bottom on the votive cup (drawing b). The peel-off tape usually has a red liner. Remove the liner from the tape. Line up the edge of one of the wraps over the adhesive and press down to secure it. Wrap the paper tightly around the votive cup and apply another strip of tape under the unsecured edge of the paper (drawing c). Remove the tape liner and press the adhesive to the votive cup. It may take a few tries to get the hang of it, so don't worry if your first tries come out a little lopsided. Just tear away the paper and start again. The more you do, the easier they become.

a

b

Double-Sided Tape

c

Add Strip of Tape

4. The matchbox is very easy to wrap. To make a wrap, you'll need the measurement for the height and the measurement around three of the four sides of the matchbox (drawing d). Ultimately, you'll want to leave one of the short sides of the matchbox uncovered to expose the match strike area (a *very* important detail if you want to be able to light the matches). Cut the measurements from decorative paper and apply the wrap to the matchbox, securing it with peel-off adhesive tape.

Tips & Hints

- Leave the final placement of your favors to your wedding coordinator, caterer, or handy helpers, if you can.

- Buy candles and votive holders in bulk or use coupons from local craft stores to get the best deals.

- Any kind of paper can be used to decorate the votive cups and matchboxes. Try vintage wallpapers, old love letters, wrapping paper, or even paper doilies. Fabric works well, too.

- You can display your darling creations in many fun ways. Line up the candles on the favor table and put the matchboxes in a large, clear glass fishbowl. How about attaching the matchboxes to the sides of the candles with a personalized ribbon? Another presentation is to simply set the matchbox on top of the candle.

- Many people have aversions to strong scents. When picking out your candles, buy unscented or lightly scented votives.

Cost Comparison

Votive candle favors can cost upward of $2 each from wedding vendors. The DIY Bride version, including matchbox, costs about $1 to make.

Store Cost:	Your Cost:
$2	**$1**

BRIDESMAID *Tote*

Your bridesmaids are saints. They've endured trips to four different bridal salons, the agony of trying on 11 different gown styles, and endless debates about the merits of Tiffany blue versus robin's-egg blue. And that's just in the last week.

As a small token of thanks, pamper your pals with personalized tote bags. Perfect for the beach or strolling through the local farmer's market, this bag is an easy and economical gift to make—and something that your maids are sure to appreciate.

The bag is a great gift on its own. For something unexpected and fun, stuff it full of spa goodies or necessities for a day at the beach.

The hardest part of creating the bag is deciding on the design. You can use the same design for all of your maids or create a unique design for each. For fabulous graphics to download, go to online stock art sites (see resources on page 214) and search for suitable clip art or photos to use in your design.

Get Your Craft On:

Going Solo

This is a great project for a quiet afternoon or evening. Grab your drink of choice, put on your "guilty pleasure" music, and enjoy some crafty "me" time.

Supplies Needed:

- Canvas tote bag, available at craft stores
- Inkjet transfer paper, available at office supply stores
- Computer with a graphics program, such as Adobe Photoshop™, Adobe Illustrator™, CorelDRAW®, Microsoft® Publisher, or The Print Shop™
- Inkjet printer (laser printers will not work with this project)
- Glue gun
- Scissors
- Iron
- Towel or pillowcase
- Ribbon

DIRECTIONS

1. Open your favorite page layout or graphics program. Create a new document.

2. Create, insert, or import your desired artwork into the new document. This is the fun part! You can create any design you want. For something simple and traditional, make a monogram for each maid in your wedding colors. Looking for something more cutting edge? Shop around stock art sites such as www.iStockPhoto.com for hip and haute graphics to incorporate into your design. Are you the sentimental type? Use a cherished photo of you and your maid(s) as the design and add a favorite quote or song lyrics.

3. The next step is flipping your image on the screen. When you transfer the design to the tote bag, it will be the opposite—the reverse or mirror image of what you have on the screen (left will be right and right will be left). Each program has its own command for flipping or mirroring images in its toolbar. Refer to your program manual for specific flipping instructions. Print a test image on plain paper. Make adjustments to the design as needed.

4. Once you're satisfied with the design and how it prints, load a sheet of transfer paper into the printer. Print the design (drawing a).

5. Set the print aside to completely dry.

6. Turn on your iron. Put it on a high, cotton, no-steam setting. Let the iron heat for about 10 minutes. It needs to be very, very hot, otherwise the transfer may fail.

7. Place a towel or pillowcase or other cloth on a hard, flat surface. Don't use a padded ironing board. Place the blank tote bag onto the middle of the ironing area.

8. Place the printed transfer face down on the tote bag and align it carefully (drawing b).

9. Now, iron the back of the transfer in a circular motion. Apply constant, firm pressure for one minute, or however long your particular transfer paper recommends (drawing c).

10. Let the transfer cool completely on the tote bag.

11. After the tote bag and transfer have cooled, grasp a corner of the transfer paper and gently peel it away from the tote bag (drawing d). If you see the transfer hasn't adhered to the tote bag, smooth the transfer paper down and iron that area again. Let it cool and then remove the paper.

12. Turn on the glue gun and let it heat up.

13. Measure the length of the tote bag handles and cut ribbon to that length. Glue the ribbon to the handles with the glue gun. I use several dots of glue along the handle instead of a single line of glue under the ribbon.

14. The last step is to make two small bows and glue them to where the ribbon on the handle meets the lip of the bag. This will cover the raw edges of the cut ribbon and add a cute, feminine touch to the design.

Tips & Hints

- Buy the heaviest canvas bags you can find. Heavier fabrics handle the transfer process better than lighter fabrics.

- Blank canvas totes can be found at most craft stores and are available individually or in sets of three or more.

- Inkjet transfer sheets are excellent for other projects. Try customizing T-shirts for the bridal party or mouse pads for your techie groomsmen. Another fun use is on plain, glazed ceramic tiles from the local home improvement center for use as customized drink coasters.

- Most inkjet transfer papers have printing on the lining. The printed side is the one you want the iron to touch.

- Don't be afraid to press down hard while you're ironing. This helps push the transfer material into the fibers of the canvas bag.

- Don't let the iron linger too long in one spot. The heat of the iron will discolor the transfer or even burn it. Keep the iron moving at all times.

Cost Comparison

Bridesmaid tote bags cost upward of $40 from the major wedding retailers. This version costs less than $10.

Store Cost:	Your Cost:
$40	**$10**

RESIN *Cufflinks*

I've always thought groomsmen got short-changed in the thank-you-gift department. Seriously, how many engraved flasks, travel kits, and pocket watches does one guy really need?

So when it came time to give something nifty and unique to the guys in my wedding party, I made custom cufflinks. With a few jewelry supplies, some resin, and some great paper you can create a completely original design for about $10.

My version uses some swell scrapbook paper, but any paper or image can be used as the cufflink design.

Are your guys traditionalists? Go for a simple monogram. Sports fanatics? Use a team logo. Wild and wacky? Try a favorite picture or cartoon.

This is an easy project for beginners but it's a bit time-consuming. The resin takes a good 24 hours to completely harden, so plan ahead.

Get Your Craft On:

Going Solo

The cufflinks are easy to make. The big challenge is waiting for them to completely dry. Give yourself at least a full 24 hours for the resin and glue to dry. Plan ahead on this one!

Supplies Needed

- Cufflink findings or a tie-tack backing (can be found at most craft stores); cufflink findings are the hardware part of a cufflink that allows the face or design to attach to a shirt cuff
- Bezel cup, about 1 inch; bezel cups are small metal jewelry findings that have a raised edge. They're most often used for holding a stone in place
- Patterned paper
- Resin
- White glue
- Strong jewelry-grade adhesive, such as E6000®
- Paper cup
- Craft sticks or clean Popsicle® sticks

DIRECTIONS

1. Cut a piece of patterned paper to fit the inside of the bezel cup. Raid your local scrapbook store for awesome decorative papers. Do buy a few extra sheets of any that you plan on using, just in case you need more. Paper designs, like fashions, change every season. You don't want to get caught running out of a paper that's been discontinued. Adhere the paper to the inside with white glue. Set aside until completely dry (drawing a).

2. With the craft stick, mix the resin per the manufacturer's recommendations in the paper cup. Be sure to do this in a well-ventilated area! Pour the resin into the bezel cup, over the paper, filling it completely (drawing b). Set the cup on an even surface to cure, usually for about 24 hours. Resin dries through a chemical process called curing. The resin will become progressively harder throughout the curing process.

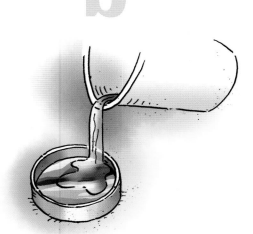

3. Your patience pays off! Once the resin has cured, glue the bezel onto the cufflink findings with jewelry adhesive (drawings c and d). They're now ready to present to your groom and groomsmen. You can find lovely (but oh-so-manly) gift boxes at party supply and craft stores for under $1.

Tips & Hints:

- Bezel cups come in a variety of shapes and sizes. I recommend staying on the smaller end of the spectrum, under 1 inch.

- Don't overmix the resin. You'll create bubbles, which are hard to get rid of once the resin is poured. If you do encounter bubbles after you've poured the resin, a straight pin will pop the bubbles, or you can use a short, quick blast of heat from an embossing gun.

- Resin is sticky, stinky goo. Protect your work surface with a layer of waxed paper and work in a well-ventilated area.

Any paper or image can be used as the cufflink design. Let your imagination run wild!

Cost Comparison

Designer resin cufflinks can easily fetch $80 in boutiques. The DIY Bride version costs about $10 to make.

Store Cost:	Your Cost:
$80	**$10**

6 Looking Back

Making Memories to Save

Just because your big day is over doesn't mean it has to be forgotten. In this chapter, I'll show you how to pull together your photos and memorabilia to create some clever projects that serve as sweet reminders of your amazing wedding. The Keepsake Display Box is perfect for prominently and stylishly showcasing your favorite pieces of wedding swag in your home. Your folks will love displaying the Photo Memento Box, and you and your hubby can amuse yourselves for years to come as you open the Time Capsule to read what your friends and family predicted for your future.

Predict The Future of Mr. & Mrs. Fletcher

1. Select a time 1, 5, 15, or 25 years ahead.

2. Write your predictions on the colored card that corresponds to the number of years ahead you want Olivia and Greg to read your message.

3. Fold the card in half and place it into the time capsule.

Not sure what to write? How about:

* How many children will they have by this date?
* Where will they be living?
* How many robots will they have in their house?
* Send a congratulatory note on reaching their anniversary.
* Offer your best advice for a happy marriage.

In Twenty Five Years ...

In Five Years ...

In Fifteen Years ...

3 kids and a dog for Greg and Olivia!

In One Year ...

TIME *Capsule*

Did you know that among your friends and family there are gifted visionaries? So clever are these individuals that they can predict the future of you and your new spouse 1, 5, 15, even 25 years away. Few will be accurate, of course, but you won't know who's right and who's wrong for years to come. Oh, the intrigue!

Instead of collecting a book of your guests' signatures that will rarely be opened after your wedding date, enlist their help in creating a time capsule that you'll open on significant dates in the future.

This time capsule is a decorated tin that houses well-wishes and predictions for the future on cards you designate to open on your 1st, 5th, 15th, and 25th anniversaries. It's a fun and interactive memento of your wedding day that can be made in under an hour for just a few dollars.

Get Your Craft On:

Going Solo

This is a great project for a quiet afternoon or evening. Grab your drink of choice, put on your "guilty pleasure" music, and enjoy some crafty "me" time.

Supplies Needed

- Decorative tin, with lid
- Decoupage medium, available at craft stores; decoupage medium is a specially formulated glue for adhering paper without buckling or distortion
- Decorative papers
- Brayer, a tool that looks like a paint roller with a rubber head, used for smoothing out papers (optional)
- Foam brush or small paintbrush
- Craft knife
- Computer with Microsoft Word
- Printer

DIRECTIONS

1. Give your tin a good scrub with soapy water and let it air dry. This helps the papers and paints stick to it and not peel away. If you're not jazzed for a plain white or silver background, paint your tin with acrylic craft paints or spray paint. Remember to let the paint completely dry before moving on to the next step.

2. To cover the outside of the tin, measure the amount of paper you'll need. Measure around the girth of the tin and add ¼ inch for overlap. Measure the height of the tin (drawing a).

3. My tin has a handle. If your tin also has a handle, cutting the holes to accommodate the handle can be a bit tricky. The best way to do this is to wrap scrap paper around the tin and use a pencil to trace where the holes should be onto the scrap (drawing b). Use this scrap paper as your template so that the holes will align properly on the decorative paper.

cut holes for handles (if necessary)

4. Cut the decorative paper to the length and height of your tin. Overlay the template on the decorative paper and trace where the holes should be. Cut the holes out and make a slit from the center of each hole to the top of the paper. This allows you to slip the paper over the handle without removing it.

5. Apply a generous and even layer of decoupage medium to the back of the decorative paper as well as to the surface of the tin (drawing c).

6. Stick the paper to the tin (drawing d). Use the brayer or your fingers to gently push down the paper and remove any wrinkles. Wipe any excess glue away with a paper towel.

7. For the lid, I cut a design from the decorative paper and applied it with decoupage medium as in steps 5 and 6.

8. Let the glue dry. This will take at least 3 hours.

9. For the cards, I printed "In 1 Year . . .," "In 5 Years . . .," "In 15 Years . . .," and "In 25 Years . . ." onto 4¼-inch by 5½-inch cardstock. Each year prints on a different color (drawing e).

Tips & Hints:

- Decorative tins can be found in all sorts of shapes and sizes at craft stores.

- Instead of a tin, use a cardboard box or an old suitcase to house your notes and predictions.

- Along with the notes from your guests, include other special mementos from your wedding day. Here are some possibilities:
  Copy of your marriage certificate
  Newspaper from the day of your wedding
  Photos of you both on your wedding day
  CDs of wedding songs from the evening
  Flowers from your bouquet

- Write a letter to your future selves: What do you wish to accomplish together by your 1st, 5th, 10th, and 25th anniversaries?

Cost Comparison

Time capsules available from wedding salons and craft stores cost around $20. This version costs under $10 and is completely customizable.

Store Cost:	Your Cost:
$20	$10

PHOTO *Memento Block*

My family members are photo fanatics. Step inside any of our homes and you'll find walls, shelves, and even entire rooms dedicated to housing and displaying our family photos. Nary a gathering goes by that isn't well-documented through dozens of snazzy snapshots and perfectly posed pics.

When it came time to come up with a little thank-you gift for my folks, a photo craft was definitely in order. However, I wanted something a little different, something that didn't need to be mounted on the wall and that could serve as part of their décor. The Photo Memento Block fit the bill quite nicely. It is inexpensive to make and an easy craft for any skill level. How easy? All you do is decorate wood blocks.

Wood blocks can be found in craft and hobby stores in a variety of sizes measuring up to 2½ inches. For this project, I wanted something a little larger, so I had a 4×4 wood post from the local home improvement center cut into blocks for a nominal fee. If you opt to do this, know that lumber sizes are not the actual measurements of the wood. I found out (the hard way) that the 4×4 lumber actually measures 3½ inches by 3½ inches. Find out the exact lumber measurements before you cut to ensure your blocks will have equal measurements on all sides.

Supplies Needed

- Wood blocks, available precut from hobby stores or custom-cut from home improvement centers.
- 1 sheet 120 grit (coarse) and 1 sheet 180 grit (medium) sandpaper
- Acrylic craft paint
- White glue, diluted with a little water
- Double-sided tape
- 2 foam brushes, 1 inch to 2 inches wide
- Cardstock or decorative papers
- Wedding photos
- Paper cutter
- Embellishments such as frames, silk flowers, crystals, and stickers
- Roll of waxed paper

DIRECTIONS

1. Sand wood blocks until they're smooth and free of any splinters or bumpy spots. If you haven't sanded wood before, don't worry; the technique is pretty straightforward. Using the coarsest grit (the lower the number of grit, the coarser the paper), rub the sandpaper along the wood in the same direction of the grain. The wood's grain refers to the natural lines that appear on the wood. If the lines go left to right, sand left to right. If they go up and down, sand in a top-to-bottom direction. The coarse-grit paper will take away the larger imperfections on the wood surface but won't make it totally smooth. To get a smooth surface, move to a higher-grit paper and, again, sand along the wood's grain. After you achieve a smooth surface, use a slightly damp paper towel to remove any wood shavings and dust from the surface of your block.

2. When working with paints and glues, I like to use waxed paper under my projects to protect my work surface. So, tear off a sheet or two of waxed paper from the roll to cover your workspace.

3. The next step is to paint your wood blocks with a background color. This can be any color you'd like. My best advice is to pick one that coordinates with the papers and pictures you'll be using on the block. When in doubt, white, black, and cream are always good choices. Squeeze a pool of paint onto the waxed paper and use one of the foam brushes to paint five of the six sides of the block. Let the first coat dry and paint those sides again, if needed. When the surface is completely dry, give the unpainted sixth side a coat of paint (and a second coat, if needed) and set it to dry (photo a).

4. Now the fun part begins! Decorate the cubes by adding decorative papers, pictures, and embellishments (photo b). To affix cardstock or papers as a background for your pictures, I recommend using a foam brush and a thin layer of thinned white glue to stick the

paper to the painted surface. Thinning glue is easy. Just add a little bit of water to a puddle of white glue poured onto your waxed-paper surface. The consistency you're aiming for is similar to a thick maple syrup—sticky but not watery. Adhering pictures to paper or paper to paper is best done with a good double-sided tape. Wet adhesives tend to buckle paper and pictures when they're stuck to a paper background. For metal, plastic, or fabric embellishments, go for hot glue. It's fast and easy, and sticks really well.

Tips & Hints

- Instead of having wood posts cut to size, you can buy children's toy blocks from the toy store. They're smaller than what I've made here, but they're readily available and require no preparation.

- Remember to leave one side without bulky embellishments. You need one flat side for the bottom of the cube.

- Some fun, interesting ideas for backgrounds are wrapping paper, scrapbook papers, your wedding invitation, fabric, sheet music from your ceremony, or a handwritten thank-you note to the recipient.

Cost Comparison

I haven't seen anything like this on the market. The cost per unit for this project was around $5.

Store Cost:	Your Cost:
—	$5

Trisha Linde
and
Gavin Burroughs

invite you to share their happiness
at their wedding

Friday, the sixteenth of May
at six o'clock

The Beach Club
Carmel By The Sea, California

KEEPSAKE *Display Box*

So, your wedding day has come and gone and the entire year you spent agonizing over every detail has paid off. But what do you have to show for it, besides a new husband and some pretty swell wedding gifts?

What happened to those fab invites you obsessed over for months? Or that one-of-a-kind cake topper you crafted by hand? What became of those amazing and outrageously expensive flowers you had imported from another country? They're all tucked away in a box in the attic or in between pages of a scrapbook, aren't they?

Gather those treasured mementos from your ceremony and reception and place them into a keepsake shadow box. Let all of those wonderful details that gave your wedding such unique personality shine brightly as an art display in your home. Enjoy them every day as a constant reminder of your utterly wonderful and beautiful wedding.

The cool thing about shadow boxes is that they provide a three-dimensional space to arrange all of your goodies. You're free to create layers, hang trinkets from the interior ceiling, add compartments, or go for simplicity. Any theme and style works, from minimalist simplicity to over-the-top opulence.

Supplies Needed:

- Shadow box (they're available in
  sizes from 4 inches by 6 inches to
  poster size; select the size that best
  fits your treasures)
- A collection of memorabilia
  and trinkets
- Straight pins and adhesives for
  mounting your items (see step 3)
- Background papers or fabrics in the
  colors of your choice
- Embellishments such as ribbon,
  glitter, buttons, matchbooks, or
  flowers (dried or silk)

DIRECTIONS

1. Select your keepsake items. Need inspiration? Include your wedding invitations, favors, bride's garter, groom's cufflinks, the cake topper, fabric from the bride's gown, place cards from the reception, a copy of the wedding vows, bride's tiara or hair accessories, photos from the honeymoon, airline tickets, or photos of the bride and groom.

2. Remove the back panel from the shadow box and cover it to create a background. You'll attach most of the memorabilia to the back panel (usually a piece of wood or heavy mat board). The panel can be altered with paper, paint, or fabric to create the perfect background for your trinkets. I glued a vintage-inspired scrapbook paper on my panel (photo a).

3. Attach your memorabilia to the back panel (photo b). How you attach your items depends on how fragile the items are and how long you'd like to display them in the box.
   Straight pins are excellent for items that are you'd like to display temporarily in the box or that you do not wish to use adhesives on.
   Double-sided foam tape adheres items to the back panel. The foam creates a permanent bond with paper items and lightweight, fragile items such as lace or flowers.
   Liquid adhesives such as glue, rubber cement, and epoxy create a permanent bond between the back panel and the item attached to it.
   Museum putty is a strong but removable plastic-like adhesive that's perfect for holding glass or ceramic pieces in place. Use it for attaching items to the inner top and bottom rims of the box.

4. Create dimension inside the box. Take advantage of the box's three-dimensional space. Some ideas for creating depth:
   Create layers—Place smaller items on top of larger ones with a little space in between. Pad the space between layers with

cardboard pieces, cotton batting, or tissue paper to give extra dimension.

Add shelves or boxes—Use chipboard or cardboard to create places to mount special items. Attach the shelves or boxes to the back panel with a strong adhesive and cover them with coordinating paper or paint.

Use the inside rims—Hang items from the top inside ledge of the box and place items on the inner bottom ledge. Think of these as the ceiling and floor of your box space.

5. For a little extra pizzazz, add some embellishments to the trinkets and treasures on display. Flowers from the bride's bouquet, ribbon, lace, rhinestones, glitter, buttons, and fabric all make lovely additions.

6. Once you have your items in place, double-check the layout for any missing items, items that need extra support, exposed adhesives or seams, or lint and unsightly fluff that you don't want displayed. When everything's OK, replace back panel. Display your beautiful treasures on a wall or tabletop.

Tips & Hints

- To help preserve your mementos, keep your display box out of direct sunlight. The sun will not only fade your treasured items but also deteriorate adhesives and fragile items.

- Watch for sales and coupons at large craft stores. They often carry quality display boxes that are perfect for this project.

Cost Comparison

Custom-designed memorabilia boxes cost upward of $100 for a small collection of keepsakes. Our version costs about $30 for the shadow box, paper, and embellishments.

Store Cost:	Your Cost:
$100	**$30**

RESORCES

I've put together a list of some of my favorite retailers, manufacturers, and websites to help you find all of the supplies called for in this book.

General Craft Stores
Many of the supplies used in the book came from my local big-box craft stores. Many of the biggies frequently offer 40-percent-off to 50-percent-off coupons, making them great resources for quality craft supplies on the cheap.
A. C. MOORE
www.acmoore.com
JO-ANN FABRIC AND CRAFT STORES
www.joann.com
MICHAELS STORES
www.michaels.com
SAVE ON CRAFTS
www.save-on-crafts.com

Crystals, Rhinestones, Jewelry Findings
DREAMTIME CREATIONS
www.dreamtimecreations.com
Excellent prices and a wide selection of flat-back rhinestones.
FIRE MOUNTAIN GEMS
www.firemountaingems.com
The go-to spot for all things jewelry. I bought most of the supplies for the tiara and earrings here, and was impressed by their excellent customer service.

JAN'S JEWELRY SUPPLIES
www.jansjewels.com
Great for unusual jewelry findings, such as the cufflink bezels.
LUCY'S FASHION FABRICS AND TRIMS
www.lucysfabrics.com
I loved Lucy's selection of rhinestone buckles, and the service was outstanding.

Fabric and Textiles
DENVER FABRICS
www.denverfabrics.com
A wide selection of textiles at very reasonable prices. Even with shipping costs, I found Denver to be more reasonable than many of my local sources.
WORLD MARKET
www.worldmarket.com/home.jsp
The fabric canopy for the altar project was a curtain from World Market. They have fun and fabulous home décor at reasonable prices. Check here for vases, bamboo poles, and glassware.

Flowers
These were the top recommendations from my DIY wedding community:
2G ROSES
www.freshroses.com
The helpful folks and excellent prices at 2G Roses make this an excellent resource for DIY flowers.

FIFTY FLOWERS
www.fiftyflowers.com
FLOWERS BY FLOWERBUD.COM
www.flowerbud.com
GROWER'S BOX
www.growersbox.com
KELLEY WHOLESALE FLORIST
www.kelleywholesale.com

Garden Centers and Home Improvement Stores
Nearly every town has a major-chain home and garden center, making them convenient and affordable spots to find building supplies and tools.
HOME DEPOT
www.homedepot.com
LOWE'S
www.lowes.com

Millinery Supplies
JUDITH M
www.judithm.com
One of the best places in the United States to find veil netting.
LACIS
www.lacis.com
A lovely spot to buy metal headbands for tiaras and flower girl hair accessories.

Paper and Cardstock
I have a mix of retailers and manufacturers in this category. Although many manufacturers don't sell directly to the public, their websites are an excellent

spot to check out what's new and exciting in product offerings. They also list retailers where you can find their products. The retail shops have been recommended and reliable sources throughout my entire crafting career.

ANNA GRIFFIN, INC.

www.annagriffin.com

BAZZILL BASICS PAPER, INC.

www.bazzillbasics.com

CHATTERBOX, INC.

www.chatterboxinc.com

DICK BLICK

www.dickblick.com

FOOF-A-LA BY AUTUMN LEAVES

www.autumnleaves.com

KI MEMORIES, INC.

www.kimemories.com

MAIDO

378 Santana Row, #1125

San Jose, CA 95128

408-213-1985

Great selection of Japanese papers

MY MIND'S EYE

www.mymindseye.com

PAPER PRESENTATION

www.paperpresentation.com

PAPER SOURCE

www.paper-source.com

PEARL RIVER

www.pearlriver.com

Great selection of Chinese papers

Ribbon

Great ribbon shops abound online. Check out these fine retailers for beautiful, affordable ribbons in nearly every color imaginable.

CHEAP RIBBONS

www.cheapribbons.com

JKM RIBBON & TRIMS

www.jkmribbon.com

M & J TRIMMING

www.mjtrim.com

THE RIBBON SPOT

www.theribbonspot.com

Rubber Stamps

ALL NIGHT MEDIA

www.plaidonline.com/apANM.asp

ASTA ARTS

www.astaarts.com

These great folks make the best hip, cool, and funky stamps.

IMPRESS RUBBER STAMPS

www.impressrubberstamps.com

I loved Impress for their great selection of fun and elegant stamps. They also have a very good selection of accessories and they even make custom stamps.

MAGENTA RUBBER STAMPS

www.magentastyle.com

SIMON'S STAMPS

www.simonstamp.com

RED CASTLE

www.red-castle.com

Tealights and Candles

CUDGE.NET

www.cudge.net

GENERAL WAX AND CANDLE COMPANY

www.genwax.com

IKEA

www.ikea.com

If you're lucky enough to live near an Ikea, do check them out for candles. They have some of the best prices anywhere.

Vases and Glassware

CRATE AND BARREL

www.crateandbarrel.com

EBAY

www.ebay.com

IKEA

www.ikea.com

WEST ELM

www.westelm.com

INDEX

Note: Bold page numbers indicate that illustrations or photos appear. (When only one number of a page range is bold, illustrations or photos appear on one or more of the pages.)